Praise for Believe in Love

"This book is beautifully written by two connected souls, sharing their life experience to helps others find their own path. It's a compelling and authentic explanation of how the world around us is intertwined with who we are, and more importantly who we want to become.
And …..my own journey is
Five years ago, I had a mild scepticism tinged with mild intrigue on Feng Shui. I had a lovely home, great career, fab friends everything in fact, except a soul mate. I met Dawn in a business capacity and as a result ended up having my home expertly Feng Shuied. Specifically looking for my soul mate I was told my "love area" was quite literally the dog toilet in the garden! Swiftly rectified I met my soul mate a week later. Hard to escape the evidence as Dawn and Lionel illustrate.

Me and my now wonderful husband are about to make a life changing move to a farm………………. and yes it will be defined for negative predecessor energy, assessed for geo stress and designed along the Feng Shui principal.
Read their book and find your inner peace."

Kay Allen

"To anyone who thinks they have left it too late to find true happiness and their soul mate, or to anyone who thinks they are not worthy of such joy, this is a must read. Dawn's honesty as she speaks from her heart is uplifting and gives hope. Lionel's warm and loving words wrap around you in a comforting embrace. The promise of a fulfilled life is within us all, we just need to know how to look within ourselves to discover who we truly want to be. This book has the power to spark a new life for us all."

Amanda Redwood, Health and Wellbeing Writer, Cheshire

"This book is a masterpiece of not only finding your soul mate by learning more about yourself and the people around you but also how to maintain happy relationships. It is written in an enjoyable way, which makes complex information easy to understand. The combination of spiritual insights and practical exercises makes this book the perfect read for everyone – no matter if you are new to the concepts such as Astrology, Feng Shui and Heart Freedom or if you have touched on them in the past. You will face your fears, find out more about yourself and will understand the people around you on a deeper level. After reading this book you will have the feeling you know Dawn and Lionel personally. This is the book everybody is waiting for!"

**Christine Michaelis, Vice President of the European Start-up Association,
founder of the Creative Start-Up Academy and the Digital Nomad Town**

"Dawn and Lionel have created a beautiful spiritual road map for travelling through this one sacred life in pursuit of erotic bliss. If you are ready to open your heart and mind to love and sexual fulfilment, this guide will help you find your soul mate. Essential reading for those who want to learn to live with intent and purpose; seek out sensuality and pleasure; and find balance and harmony with their ideal partner."

Michelle Ewen, Storytelling Specialist, Cheshire

BELIEVE IN LOVE

Three Steps to Finding Heaven on Earth

1. Dare
2. Discover
3. Deepen

By
Dr Dawn De Vivre MBE & Lionel Palatine

CONTENTS

Praise for Believe in Love 3

Welcome 9

Our Calling 11

Introducing the Authors – Dawn and Lionel 13

Dawn 15

Lionel 17

Who is this book for? 18

How to use this book: 18

STEP 1 – DARE
Dare to be Different – How Dawn Made Her Dreams Come True 21
Dedication 23

Chapter 1: Dare to be Different 25

Chapter 2: From Negative to Positive 35

Chapter 3: New Life: New Home 41

Chapter 4: Erotic Dreams 47

Chapter 5: The Shock 57

Chapter 6: Tantric Bliss 63

Chapter 7: The Hanky Panky Pond 67

Chapter 8: Heavens Edge 71

Chapter 9: Sexual Transmutation – The Sacred Trilogy 77

STEP 2 – DISCOVER
Practices to Discover Inner Happiness and Awaken Your Hidden Powers by Lionel and Dawn 85
Dedication 87

Chapter 1: How to Divine with Cards to Discover Inner Happiness 89

Chapter 2: How to use Divining Rods 93

Chapter 3: How to use a Divining Pendulum 97
Chapter 4: Divining with Your Body 103
Chapter 5: How to Discover Your True InnerNature............. 105
Chapter 6: How to live in a healthy home 113
Chapter 7: How to Live in a Happy Home 131
Chapter 8: How to Create the Life of Your Dreams - Dream Board Creation.. 147
Chapter 9: How to be a Pearl Fisher 153
Chapter 10: How to Calm Your Mind with Mantras 155
Chapter 11: How to Discover Inner Happiness with Chanting 159
Chapter 12: How to Connect with Nature 163
Chapter 13: How to Experience Tantra.................................. 165
Chapter 14: How to Nurture Your Spirit 167
Chapter 15: How to Transform Darkness to Light 175
Chapter 16: How to Find Your Soul Tribe.............................. 183
Chapter 17: How to Balance Your Mind, Body, and Soul with Ayurveda 189

STEP 3 – DEEPEN
Lionel takes you on a journey to help you make your dreams come true.... 199
Chapter 1: Lionel's Perspective: *Introducing Heart Freedom* 203
Chapter 2: Seven Steps to Success.. 213
Chapter 3: Intentions and Objectives 217
Chapter 4: Finding Love 219
Chapter 5: The Fear of Loss 223
Chapter 6: Barriers 225
Chapter 7: Motivation.. 227
Chapter 8: Mind of Love.. 229
Chapter 9: One True Love 231

Chapter 10: To Love or Not to Love 233

Chapter 11: Beliefs 235

Chapter 12: Are You Worthy of Love? 237

Chapter 13: Seek Love 239

Chapter 14: Your Own Love Beliefs 241

Chapter 15: Learning to Love 243

Chapter 16: Clear Yourself for Love 245

Chapter 17: Let Love Flow 247

Chapter 18: What Sort of Love do You Want? 249

Chapter 19: Your Love Type 251

Chapter 20: Know Thy Own Love 253

Chapter 21: Building Heart Freedom 255

Chapter 22: Creating Heart Freedom 261

Conclusion 263

Reconnecting With Your TrueSelf 265

100 Questions 267

Lifestyle Self-Assessment Questionnaire 275

Glossary of Terms 301

Lionel Palatine 309

Dr. Dawn De Vivre MBE 313

Offerings 317

Welcome

Welcome to our Trilogy of Life and Love

Within the pages of this book, we share with you our journey of discovery. It has taken us 40 years of life learning to discover the secret of relationship bliss and we want to share it with you and millions of others around the world to inspire hope and to create harmony and happiness.

Our book invites you to explore your deepest thoughts and desires to discover inner happiness and to find your meaning of life. It's split into three parts: **Dare, Discover and Deepen.** These are critical to your journey to inner happiness and to ignite your hidden powers.

Dare: Dawn shares her dreams of finding a sexually and spiritually blissful relationship, and her journey to discover a soul mate.

Discover: Dawn and Lionel teach you how to discover practices that will unleash your inner happiness.

Deepen: Lionel shares his journey to discover unconditional love and his understanding of what love is, from a man's perspective. Lionel determines what you need to consider on your journey to make your dreams come true, to deepen your understanding of love and find Heart Freedom.

Our passion is to awaken the conscious collaboration of people all over the world to experience pure bliss. You can experience passionate purpose and develop the sense of pure bliss when you find your true soul mate.
Undo the damage of ignorance and create extraordinary healing to guide your path to love.

Our Calling

Our calling is to share our experiences of relationship bliss with the world. We are so blessed to have found a harmonic balanced fulfilling relationship and it is our hearts' desire that you discover yours too.

We want our books to be catalysts, connecting and enabling kindred spirits who have a passion to make a difference, unite and create a better world. A vibrant community of change makers who dare to be different. Together we can truly make this world a wonderful place to live, for us, our children, our grandchildren, our grandchildren's children, for everyone, for ever more.

In this era of discovery, we can all be on a voyage to uncover our true self, to feel alive and to understand how to live healthy, happy, balanced lives. We live and teach our beliefs, that there are three areas of our lives we need to focus on to achieve this harmony; finding emotional freedom, creating physical health, and being spiritually connected.

Allow us to take you on a journey of self-discovery and to remove self-doubts. We invite you to free your heart and open your mind to find your purpose in life, because when you understand your purpose, you can live your life as 'you', your authentic self. Only then can you find your inner happiness and experience a new dawn for yourself.

Introducing the Authors – Dawn and Lionel

Dawn and Lionel achieved pure contentment from helping others and guiding them on their journey to find inner happiness. Their combined experience and knowledge of business, life and relationships was extensive and their exuberance and excitement for peace and joy was well known.

The couple had spent many years and invested a lot of their time and money working towards understanding relationships so that they could help others obtain happiness. They passionately knew that you cannot be happy unless you know the reason you are here on Earth and what excites you and gets your juices flowing.

Dawn passed away early in 2022, only seven months after being diagnosed with cancer. Preferring to live life on her terms, she refused anything other than organic treatments and died peacefully in Lionel's arms. Her last wishes included a natural burial in Wild Spirit Woods which has since become a true memorial to the love that shone out from her soul. Her memory lives on in many people's hearts and her wishes continue to be fulfilled through Lionel's continued efforts and the spiritual connectedness they shared.

Their love, understanding and particularly their relationship programs are considered amongst the best available and the attitude to life it creates is infectious.

Discover your happiness

Lionel and Dawn's belief that the meaning of everyone's life (our raison d'être) is:

1 – To find your purpose, your soul's yearning
2 – To find your passion, your gifts and talents
3 – To find your power - serve others to help you find your inner happiness (Joie de Vivre)

Lionel can be contacted for consultations at:
lionel@lionelpalatine.com

Dawn

Dawn's spark to search for inner happiness was ignited when speaking in Singapore on a trade mission with the British Government in 2003. It was here she met Giselle Rufer, Founder of Delance Swiss Watches. Giselle also spoke, her empowering talk was entitled 'Time for Women'.

Working predominantly in the construction industry, which still remains a male dominated sector, Dawn was constantly being immersed in an environment filled with masculine energy (yang). At the age of 45 Dawn decided to embark on a journey of discovery, to find her inner feminine energy (yin) and bring balance to her out of balance being.

Giselle's words remained with Dawn as her pioneering mind mixed Feng Shui and gender balance. Dawn later found herself travelling the world delivering a different type of speech – these were dynamic speeches entitled 'Dare to be Different'. She presented them with passion sharing her knowledge of Life and Leadership and how the eastern art of Feng Shui transformed her life and riches.

Several years after this initial spark, Dawn achieved her goal and found balance. She also discovered a yin-yang balanced man (Lionel) and then found her true physical, emotional, and spiritual bliss.

Dawn's purpose was to inspire joie de vivre pour tout le monde (the joy of living for all the world), to allow her personal vibrancy to inspire others to think differently, to evoke deep inner happiness, and to guide others to live in a healthy, happy, sustainable world. She contributed by being an exuberant guiding light especially on stage which made her feel illuminated, inspired, and free.

BELIEVE IN LOVE

Her heroes were her husband Lionel, Gandhi, her two daughters and her Feng Shui teacher Robert Gray.

Lionel

Lionel has always loved reading and at the age of 14 he acquired a book that transformed his life. The book contained a methodology of living to bring harmony, health, and happiness to life. Lionel studied it many times over and started to implement the practice it taught every day.

So, in 1973 this tender teenager 'Dared to be Different' and has continued with this practice throughout his life, his love of people and in particularly women has taken him in many directions. Lionel understands that we live in an unfair world and passionately wants to help people help themselves to become balanced.

He believes that a conscious world would be happier, more connected, more respectful, and more trusting. His work reflects his vision by bringing the above elements together. Lionel's desire is to live in a world where everyone works together, towards clear objectives, and for organizations to create greater good for people and our planet.

Lionel's purpose is driven by personal connections to help others gain a greater understanding of self-awareness, and to create harmony. His mission in life is to help others focus on their unrealized powers and to unleash their full potential. He does this through his contributions to guiding others to help themselves be happier.

He praises, respects and graces the teachings of Mahatma Gandi, Jiddu Krishnamurti, and Yogi Bhajhan, along with the music of Bob Marley, John Lennon, and others. His heroes are his beloved children Lauren and Antony.

Who is this book for?

This book is for everyone. For both women and men to discover their Joie de Vivre (their Joy of Living).

You may be single, or in a relationship where you feel you could truly benefit from a greater understanding of each other, or you may be in a difficult relationship at this time. By understanding your authentic self, you will be able to nurture your relationships with your own spirit, your lover, friends, family, even your colleagues. When you give love, the Universe gives it back in abundance.

How to use this book:

This book is to inspire you to take yourself on a deep meaningful journey of inner exploration. To find happiness and to realize your hidden powers.

We share with you our life experiences and guidance on how to achieve and experience an ecstatic new life full of joy that will lead you to find your soul mate and true happiness.

In the first part of this trilogy 'Dare' Dawn shares her journey of self-discovery by dreaming of a different world and daring to be different, stepping into her true authentic self.

In the 'Discover' part of our trilogy we share our 'how to' ideas, allowing you to open your mind to new ways of thinking, and to explore new skills to bring you health, happiness, and harmony.

In the 'Deepen' part of this trilogy Lionel inspires you to consider your true self; in this section you will be asked to reveal more about yourself.

The end of this book marks the beginning of your journey of

self-discovery as we share with you two exercises. These will allow you to identify the areas of your life which are not working and those that are. The questions we have created will allow you to get to know yourself better and to live every day authentically.

STEP 1 – DARE
Dare to be Different – How Dawn Made Her Dreams Come True

Dedication

Chapter 1 - Dawn's Journey of Discovery

Chapter 2 - From Negative to Positive

Chapter 3 - New Life – New Home

Chapter 4 - Erotic Dreams

Chapter 5 - The Shock

Chapter 6 - Tantric Bliss

Chapter 7 - Hanky Panky Pond

Chapter 8 - Heaven's Edge

Chapter 9 - Sexual Transmutation Review of Part 1 by Deana Stone

Dedication

"The Dare section of this book is dedicated to my soul mate, my twin flame, my lover, my best friend, to Lionel. The man who knew we were meant to be together from the day we met. He has taught me so much about the trilogy of life. He is my guiding light; my teacher and he has shown me how to become a balanced human being.

Lionel, thank you for your patience, thank you for your love, thank you for taking me and travelling with me on this magical mystical journey of living in pure tantric bliss.

Life with you is truly Heaven on Earth. I love you." Dawn xx

Chapter 1
Dare to be Different

Whilst on holiday in Koh Samui, Thailand I remember meeting a lady who was so excited to share her discovery of Geopathic Stress. The lady raved about this so-called negative earth energy, she said that we must never sleep on it as it causes illness, disease and even cancer.

Well, I listened to her and thought she had lost the plot. I thought the earth energies and magnetism she spoke of which negatively impacted our health was rubbish.

I was married to my first husband at the time and he too agreed that it sounded like rubbish. This event took place when I was 37 years old. Things started to happen in my life after this 'meeting' which eventually set me on a personal voyage of discovery.

At the age of 38, I was happily married with two beautiful daughters, one aged eight, the other aged six. My husband and I decided now was the right time to move from living in the town to settling in the countryside. We pictured a small holding in an idyllic location, a place where our girls could ride ponies and grow up connected to nature. A place to inspire creativity, a place we could breathe in fresh air. We envisioned our forever home.

We found an amazing property situated on the backbone of a hill called The Cloud, close to the beautiful market town of Congleton, in the county of Cheshire in England. It was exactly what we had dreamed of. Looking at the surrounding area, there were plenty of places to explore. We saw that the property was just five hundred metres away from the Neolithic standing stones known as The Bridgestone's.

Our offer was accepted, and we simply couldn't wait to move in. The day finally came for us to leave behind our town life and my family moved into our new home with all our belongings together with our gorgeous dogs; Tiny, Titch, Molly and Simba. Not long after moving in we got the ponies as planned. We called them Misty, Robbie, and Ginger Pop. To us, and to those looking in at our new home environment, everything seemed perfect, but oh my, little did we know what was in store for us.

My husband and I started to disagree on things. Both my husband's and my health deteriorated. I used to run five miles a day, but since moving to our new home my knees troubled me. I had to stop running. I started to put on weight. My husband experienced a dislocated shoulder and had to have an operation to fix it. What was going on?

There seemed to be an air of grumpiness in the house. What could I do? Where could I go for help? I started to research and ask questions. I wasn't really too sure what I was looking for, but I knew I wanted something to help remove the negativity and to restore the balance. I found a magazine called 'Feng Shui for Modern Living', looking at its contents, it seemed to offer what I was looking for. As I flicked through the bright and colourful pages, I became fascinated. I read articles describing how the energy within the house you live in could affect your health, your wealth, your relationships, and your general wellbeing.

Oh, la la, I wanted to know more. On the back of the magazine there was an advertisement for a course run by an organization called 'The Feng Shui Academy', headed by a gentleman called Robert Gray. His credentials looked good, and the course was in Buxton. This spa town is only thirty minutes from my home – it was meant to be, I thought to myself. Without hesitation I booked myself on a weekend foundation course in Feng Shui.

Chapter 1: Dare to be Different

'Wow, wow, wow'. To say I was enlightened and amazed by what I learned would be an understatement.

The course was a 'taster course' to introduce a year-long Feng Shui Practitioners Course. On the taster course we learned little bits about a lot of subjects and learned about the three main energies of Feng Shui, which are:

Heavens Energy – Astrological energy from the sun, the moon, and the stars.
Human Energy – Influenced by us human beings and the previous occupants of the house.
Earth Energy – Magnetic frequencies that resonate from the earth.

Some of the subjects we learned on the weekend were about Predecessor Energy, this is how the energy of the previous occupants becomes imprinted within the fabric of the house. So, for example, if the occupants were not happy for any reason this could be disruptive for the next occupants.

We learned about symbolism and how works of art can affect the energy in our homes. We learned about the psychology of colour and lighting and how they affect our mood and wellbeing.

For me, the best experience over the weekend was learning a new skill. I learned to divine with divining rods (also called dowsing with dowsing rods). Divining is the skill of identifying something that is invisible to the eye using either a pendulum or a pair of divining rods. We were learning this skill on the course so we could detect earth energies that can affect our health.

BELIEVE IN LOVE

I didn't want the weekend to end; I wanted to delve further into the study of Feng Shui and learn all there was to know. When I returned home with such an excitable spring in my step, I exuded joy as I told my husband what I'd learned and about my new-found skill. He was not impressed and thought it was all rubbish and that it couldn't be scientifically proven. I challenged him and asked the girls to help me in an experiment to find items that were invisible to us. I wanted to prove to him that divining worked.

I went into our kitchen and set up the experiment. I put ten mugs upside down on the kitchen floor. I then taught my two daughters, how to divine with rods. I explained to my husband what we were going to do. The girls and I would leave the kitchen and whilst we were out, he would put a coin under one of the ten mugs on the floor. I explained to him that we would then find which mug the coin was hidden under, by dowsing for it.

So, we did it. My daughters and I went out of the room and my husband put a coin under the mug. We came back into the kitchen and asked our dowsing rods, "please show us the mug with the coin underneath it".

Every time, all three of us located the coin... ten out of ten times! My husband was baffled and said it must be magnetism, magnetic forces from the metal rods to the coin. I challenged him to use something nonconductive, so he used a cork from a wine bottle and a tangerine. No matter what objects he put under the mugs my daughters and I found them every time.

My husband still wouldn't accept that it was anything but luck.

Chapter 1: Dare to be Different

My daughters were natural diviners, and we used our new divining skills when we needed them in everyday life. We found lost items such as car keys, even missing school blazers.

One Sunday we were due to go to a gymkhana with the ponies, but we could not find the horse box keys anywhere. "Mum use the divining rods," my daughter exclaimed, so I did and found the keys in a pile of straw in a stable. Wow!

OK, now back to our home's negative energy issue.

I divined our home for negative earth energies and found that we had a strong Geopathic Stress line going diagonally through our bed cutting through my legs and my husband's shoulder. This alarmed and frightened me. Maybe this could explain my husband's shoulder injury and my painful knees.

I thought back to the lady I had met at Koh Samui, I was so sorry that I'd been so quick to have dismissed her claims about Geopathic Stress. I wished I'd opened my mind to find out more, but at that time my mind was closed. Knowing what I know now, I bet we'd have had some wonderful conversations.

This made me think of checking out my mum and dad's house as my dad had died of cancer. I checked their house and found that the location where my dad used to sleep had two strong crossing Geopathic Stress lines. The lines crossed where my dad's neck was situated. My dad died of a cancer called myeloma that attacked his vertebrae and his bones, the first vertebrae to disintegrate was the one in his neck.

I was in shock, and I must admit I was scared of the consequences of what I had found. I read the reference book recommended to me by our teacher, Robert Gray, called 'Are You Sleeping in A Safe Place?' by Rolfe Jordan. No matter whom I spoke to about Feng Shui, Geopathic Stress, or the art of divining, all my friends, my family and, most of all, my husband thought I was mad.

What could I do?
I believed in what I was finding. I found evidence of it.
My divining skills confirmed it.

The reference book confirmed a study in Germany of 5000 cancer cases where 4995 of the patients were found to be sleeping on Geopathic Stress lines. It must be true. Oh wow, was I challenged.

I had to do something, so I booked to complete the Feng Shui Academy Practitioner Training Course to learn more.

Several days later I was chatting to the newsagent who delivered our papers. He told me about an 85-year-old man who lived in our town who had the skills to remove the negative earth energies from our home. I was overjoyed, not only did the newsagent listen to what I was telling him without dismissing my words, but he knew of someone else who also believed in the earth's energies. I was keen to see this person, so my newsagent took me to meet him.

The elderly gentleman, with his unique skills, agreed to come to my home to remove the negative energies using a copper rod grid. He divined for all the negative earth energy lines around the outside of our home and whenever he found one, he hammered a small piece of copper tubing into the ground. These pieces of tubes were just simple 15mm diameter copper tubing, the same as plumbers use.

Chapter 1: Dare to be Different

The copper seemed to be placed every three metres like a grid around the house. When he had finished, he and I divined again to see if we could find any negative earth energies. There were none present. The negative energies had gone. Yippee!

I explained what I had done that day to my husband, my friends, and my family and once again they thought I was talking rubbish. But guess what? We became healthier and I soon started to run again. The house did not have the grumpy feel about it anymore.

I started the Feng Shui Practitioners training in Buxton and my tutor wanted a house to use as a case study. Guess who offered? That's right, me.

We soon had 20 Feng Shui students evaluating our home. Oh, I was so excited.

On that day, I remember our teacher becoming invigorated because he had found a powerful positive energy line, a ley line, running through our house. It ran straight through my home office and my desk where I sat and spent lots of time. The excitement amongst the budding Feng Shui group was ecstatic. Ley lines are powerful electromagnetic earth energies that flow in various directions. They're an ancient wisdom that circle the globe. They can be good or bad depending on the direction of the energy and the purpose of your goal. Many churches and significant constructions in ancient times were built on crossing energy points and today they remain important regarding the flow of health, wealth, and happiness in general. Oh, how happy and honoured I was to have one run through my home. How blessed my family were.

Robert also taught us how to divine maps and plans of houses with a pendulum divining tool to find both positive and negative earth energy lines. With excitement bubbling yet again I told my family and friends and my husband. I don't need to tell you what their response was – I think you can guess.

I even overheard one of my more distant family members describing me as eccentric. Who me? No way.

Even when we went on holidays abroad, I took my enthusiasm for Feng Shui with me. I was hooked, it was a big part of my life.

One year we travelled to Mauritius for a family holiday, and I was keen to use my new divining skills in a completely new place. I divined a map of Mauritius to find positive earth energies. I did this by using a crystal pendulum divining method. *(In Step 2 DISCOVER we tell you how to divine using rods and pendulums.)*

Mauritius simply oozes beauty; you just can't help falling in love with its enchantment. So, looking for its most auspicious place was going to be tough – or so I thought. By trawling over the map with the point of the rose quartz crystal pendulum I asked, "show me positive auspicious earth energy". Over one point of the map my pendulum began to spiral in a frenzied manner. Oh, la la, what had I discovered?

Chapter 1: Dare to be Different

I pointed to the place on the map and said to my husband that I would like us all to go there. It was inland near the centre of Mauritius a long way from our hotel.

At first my husband was dismissive – no surprise there. He said, "no, we are not going, that place is in the middle of nowhere, it's in the wilderness". After my constant requesting and excitement, he agreed. I could have been worried that when we got there, there'd be nothing to see, but I knew deep inside that it was going to be special, I had faith in the pendulum and my power to divine. I was so pleased and so appreciative of my husband amusing me with my request.

We piled into a taxi not knowing what to expect – I was thrilled, my daughters were too. My husband remained as skeptical as ever. After a hot and sticky ride, we arrived at our destination and oh my, it was breath-taking. My little family found ourselves at the top of a mountain where the most beautiful Hindu Temple was located, adjacent to a wonderful lake. The energy of the place was peaceful and calm. Many people were praying and chanting and meditating there; they were sending offerings to the gods by placing flowers on leaves and floating them out on the lake. What a beautiful experience.

I sincerely thanked my husband for listening to me and being a part of my adventure. The sacred site I discovered is called Ganga Talao at the Grand Bassin Crater Lake in Mauritius. We would not have found this place if it were not for my new skill of map divining.

Chapter 2
From Negative to Positive

My voyage of discovery and appetite to gain more skills did not stop. Not only did I complete the Feng Shui Academy Practitioners Course, but I also indulged in the following courses between 2003 and 2007:
Clear Your Clutter with Feng Shui - with Karen Kingston in Bali
Space Clearing and Advanced Space Clearing - with Karen Kingston in Bali
Feng Shui Astrology - with John Sandifer in London
Feng Shui Master Practitioners Course - with Lillian Too's Institute of Feng Shui in Malaysia
Unleash the Power Within - with Anthony Robbins in London

I was like a sponge; I wanted to learn as much as possible about the unseen energies that affect our lives.

When I was 46 years old, the business I had founded made a serious loss. The year before the loss (2004) I had learned the art of Clutter Clearing; a technique to remove anything you no longer need, to remove objects that drain energy from you. Clutter can result in confusing energy that can block the natural flow of energy. I knew the right decision for my business was to use the techniques I had learned and within days we went from having two hundred filing cabinets to a more manageable fifty. I also researched the previous owners of the building and the site where we worked from, and to my horror I found out that they had gone bust and closed. The site had negative predecessor energy in it.

I instinctively knew what I had to do to save the future of my business. I booked one of Karen Kingston's top practitioners to come and 'Space Clear' our building. (*You'll learn more about this in Part 3.*) This top practitioner was Beverley Wood, a building biologist, RIBA architect and expert Space Clearer, sometimes referred to as an Atmospheric Cleanser.

I will never forget the gossip going around in my business. "Dawn is performing naked rituals on Sunday." "Dawn is dancing naked to connect with the nature spirits." I bet they had a blast conjuring up all kinds of images.

I thought the whispers around the office were hilarious. I just allowed everyone to think what they wanted as I had a deep inner knowing that this would change the flow of our future success. To let everyone know my plans, and for it not to be a shock, I explained to everyone what was going to happen in the team brief. The Monday morning following the Space Clearing, the staff arrived for work. They had to walk over thousands of flower petals at each entrance where they were greeted by flower offerings on plates. The consensus from everyone was that the whole building felt lighter, happier, and more pleasant. It was as if the sun was shining on the inside. Huge thanks to Beverley's amazing work.

I also used my divining skills and earth healing skills to dowse over the five-acre site for Geopathic Stress. Myself and my wonderful team member Kerri Rendell completed this detection work and placed a copper grid to clear away the negativity we found. I also allowed Robert Gray and a team of Feng Shui for Business students, to come down and use my company as a case study for learning.

Our offices were dressed in white walls, red chairs, and red filing cabinets – red and white were our company colours. I'll never forget Robert's first reaction when he walked in, "Oh Dawn you are stressing out all your team with too much yang!" Ouch.

Chapter 2: From Negative to Positive

Robert gave me clear instructions on how to calm down the office environment and to make it more conducive to work in. This included:

- Blue carpets (representing water flowing)
- Yellow/ochre walls (great for communication)
- Install uplighters instead of the headache inducing fluorescent tubes, and
- Install pictures of nature on the walls.

Wow! What a difference his advice made. Word quickly got around, and we caught the attention of the press. I never imagined it would lead to such interest, I genuinely did what I did to help my business grow by removing past negativity – that was reward enough for me. The Sunday Times visited to do an article on how we had transformed our business by investing in our internal environment. I loved the article; I was starting to spread the word! Over the following three years my business went from loss to profit, in fact it doubled in profit every year. My team completed their annual Staff Satisfaction Survey, and their happiness factor went from a sad 60% satisfied to over 85% satisfied. Amazing.

During this time of transformation from negative to positive, I joined the UK Feng Shui Society as part of the Executive Committee. I was so inspired by Feng Shui and felt such incredible gratitude that I just wanted to help them fly and be able to promote Feng Shui into every household. I rebranded the society, created a new website for them and developed a new strategy.

I was completely convinced by Feng Shui, yet my family, friends and now my work colleagues were not. No matter how I tried to explain the concepts of these invisible energies and the art of Feng Shui, no one seemed to understand me. I felt alone. I felt criticized. The person who criticized me the most was my husband.

I will never forget nights out at dinner parties where I would talk of Feng Shui and my husband would make comments, poking fun at me, resulting in others laughing at me. Previously our nights out were fun, people would laugh with me, but now the atmosphere at parties felt alien to me, it wasn't right. I wasn't hurting anyone, in fact quite the opposite. This constant criticism and disbelief by my family, friends and my team made me review my life. To my mind, Feng Shui had renewed my spirit; it had renewed the health of my family and my business.

My husband and I had a massive spiritual disconnection. He was very matter of fact and scientifically minded. I was a creative courageous woman on a voyage of discovery. Discovering ancient wisdom for modern times. We could no longer communicate. My whole spirit was crushed. I needed to escape.

So, on my 50th year I plucked up the courage to discuss with my husband our differences. I still loved and respected him, but we just could not live together. And so, when both our children had left home, one to university and one on a gap year, we decided to split.

I moved out of our family home. It was heart wrenching, that home had once been our dream. I knew I had to leave, but I took with me a heart and head full of treasured memories of my girls growing up in beautiful surroundings. No one can take that away from me.

My husband helped me find a new home and thankfully he was incredibly supportive. At least the very ending was not bitter or full of anger. After much house hunting, I found the home that would transform me. I just knew from the moment I saw it; this was going to be a special place for me. It was called Heather Bank Farm, nestled into a beautiful part of Congleton,

Chapter 2: From Negative to Positive

in Cheshire, England. Even its name filled me with delight, my middle name is Heather (the dictionary meaning of Heather colourful flower on a wild savage landscape') and my grandparent's surname was Banks, so somehow the house fitted me.

It will come as no surprise to you that before I moved in, I arranged for two Feng Shui Consultants to survey the house and the land, Simon Brown, and Elizabeth Wells. If this was going to be my special home, I needed to fill it with love and positivity from the very start. My new beginning in my own home. I had no idea then what the house had in store for me, and how it would come to be known as 'Blissland'.

From the age of 45 to 50 I was challenged and criticized, but I went from negative to positive. I allowed these challenges and criticisms to affect me until I found the strength and courage to overcome them. I will let you into a secret. What helped me find this strength was 'fire walking'. Yes, that's right, I indulged in a 3-day course called Unleash the Power Within hosted by Anthony Robbins which empowered me to take massive action.

Chapter 3
New Life: New Home

Soon after moving back to Congleton, I was asked by a beautiful lady called Margaret Williamson to attend a business breakfast to discuss the declining state of the town because it was becoming a ghost town. A large number of shops were closed and standing empty. I was more than happy to go along.

It was agreed at the meeting that a project was needed to rebrand our town, and everyone looked to me. "Dawn you're an international brand and marketing guru, will you head up a team to rebrand our town?" After initial consideration I exclaimed, "Yes, I will, on one condition and one condition only - and that is that we have a Feng Shui survey done on our town". This remark was followed by laughter. Here we go again!

I looked at each person in the eye and said very confidently. "I will prove to you all that this survey will help us transform our town. It will help us reveal a unique identity – the essence of our town."

Out of my own pocket, I paid for Feng Shui Master Simon Brown to come to Congleton to do the first ever Feng Shui survey on a town. Simon discovered that most of the people he met referred to Congleton as Beartown. This is a common localism in the area.

The Beartown name dates back from 1640. The market town of Congleton used to attract trade to the town with the cruel sport of bearbaiting, this involved a dancing bear entertaining visitors to the market. In 1640 the Congleton Bear died and trade in Congleton diminished. The town was saving up to buy a new bible but instead decided to purchase a new bear to once again attract new trade and keep the town prosperous.

Simon's advice to me was to resurrect the spirit of the bear. So that is exactly what I did.

The first thing I did was to set up a volunteer's team called The **BEAR** Team (**B**randing **E**mpowering **A**wakening and **R**eviving). The second thing was to present the Feng Shui 'Atmospheric Survey' results and recommendations to residents, the council, the Congleton partnership, and other stakeholders. And lastly, I presented at an assembly in every infant and junior school asking the children to write a story about 'Where has the bear been since it left Congleton?' The children's faces lit up when they learned about the bear, their innocent minds were flowing with creativity.

Following my visit to one primary school I received an email from the headmistress saying that one of her pupils had asked if we could have giant bears in our town. They'd thought how much they loved seeing the giant cows in Manchester and the rhinos in Chester and thought 'why can't Congleton have these fantastic animal sculptures?' Why not indeed?

The entrepreneurial spirit in me said a resounding yes! My wonderful team of volunteers, my BEAR team, went on to launch Bearmania which attracted over 30,000 people to our town. Shop occupancy went up to almost 90% as a result. What a great idea that little child had, I hope they know just how much of a positive ripple they caused in the town by being brave enough to talk to their headmistress about their vision.

One other recommendation from the Feng Shui survey was for the boring depressing council chamber to have its false ceiling removed to allow in natural light. Wow! What a difference that made. Now the council chambers are flooded with natural light and the council has gone on to develop many successful initiatives for the enjoyment of the town. Congleton now hosts festivals and other fun events to attract visitors.

Chapter 3: New Life: New Home

Even now, no one talks of the Feng Shui survey and yes, I was ridiculed and criticized. Yet I stood by my beliefs, and I am so proud of the results.

Why am I telling you all this? Well since I moved into my new house I was obsessed with bears. Not only due to my connection with Beartown but also with the Great Bear star constellation which is used as the basis of Feng Shui Astrology system.

We have since converted the Feng Shui astrology system into a personality profiling tool as it is so accurate. Contact lionel@lionelpalatine.com if you would like to try it out. We assess everyone's personality profile to reveal their purpose, passion, and power.

I found that my new home, set in 20 acres of land, has a 250m wide ley line running through it, which also runs through the centre of Congleton. This explains why I was obsessed with supporting the town when I moved in.

The house is elevated on a hill known as Congleton Edge and many people have said that I was like the Angel of Congleton overlooking the town from my hillside position. I set to work on making the house my home. I removed the Geopathic Stress, and I discovered positive earth energies to the right of the drive, here I installed a stone circle. At the Grand Designs Show (an exhibition of all things related to great homes) I met the inventor of Eco Dome Pods – I just loved them and installed these too. The three pods installed were named The Peace Pod, The Passion Pod (later named the Tantra Temple) and The Pee Pod (this is the functional pod!). I also installed a pond to the north of the pods.

I implemented most of the Feng Shui cures that the Feng Shui Consultants had recommended. I believe my passion of Feng Shui had catalyzed my spiritual awakening. I also believe my regular visits to the land of the gods 'Bali' had a lot to do with my spiritual awakening too.

I was in demand. The positive energy brought great guest speaking opportunities and TV appearances for me. My favourite speaking gigs were at the Leadership Masterclasses for Manchester Metropolitan University. The title of my talk was 'Organisational Spirituality—Find Your Corporate Soul'.

At each of my guest speaking gigs I'd meet many people. Those I connected with I usually offered to do their personality profiles for them and send on their results. Oh, how I loved it, and so did they.

On the 18th of August 2011 my life changed once again. I spoke at a Leadership Masterclass this day and met a delegate called Lionel. Within the first five minutes of meeting him we were talking about energy flow. I was talking about the energy of **Feng Shui,** and he was talking about the energy of **Tantra**. I was fascinated.

After my talk, he asked if I would speak at a charity event he was involved with, and I said yes. I also offered to do his personality profile. Finding out his birthday I calculated his profile numbers. I texted him his profile numbers to explain their meaning and that was that.

Chapter 3: New Life: New Home

On the 11th January 2011 I appeared on a prime-time TV programme that was aired in 20 countries. The programme really had the wow factor for millions of viewers. It was also my children's favourite programme. The programme was called **'Dawn Gibbins, the Secret Millionaire Changed My life.'**

The programme featured me volunteering with three charities in Bristol. The first was a homeless charity called The Wild Goose Café, the second was a street sex worker charity called One25 and thirdly a teenage parents' charity.

I remember watching it back and being so emotional at the end of the programme. As I walked away a sensational song was playing that touched my heart deeply. It was Feeling Good by Nina Simone.

Birds flying high you know how I feel. Sun in the sky you know how I feel.
Breeze driftin' on by you know how I feel.

It's a new dawn It's a new day
It's a new life for me, yeah.
It's a new dawn It's a new day
It's a new life for me, ooh And I'm feeling good.

Fish in the sea you know how I feel. River running free you know how I feel. Blossom on the tree you know how I feel.

It's a new dawn It's a new day
It's a new life for me

BELIEVE IN LOVE

And I'm feeling good.

Dragonfly out in the sun, you know what I mean, don't you know?
Butterflies all havin' fun, you know what I mean.
Sleep in peace when day is done, that's what I mean.
And this old world is a new world And a bold world, for me.

Stars when you shine, you know how I feel.
Scent of the pine, you know how I feel.
Oh, freedom is mine And I know how I feel.

It's a new dawn It's a new day
It's a new life for me And I'm feeling good!

Wow, how true. 2011 was a real year of transformation for me.

Chapter 4
Erotic Dreams

I decided to re-study Feng Shui with Robert Gray which took place in his and his wife Carolina's hometown in Leicestershire. The magical setting for our field studies was in Bradgate Park, a public park in Charnwood Forest. There were just five of us on the course: Olga, Natasha, Stella, Lisa, and me.

We were all so different, yet all so connected, and I developed great relationships with all of them. We had such fun and Robert excelled with his teaching yet again. Robert taught us how to talk to trees and plants and respect their presence and give gratitude to the flowers or branches before we picked them to make our wands to assist us in earth energy healing.

I really bonded with Olga, she was a runner like me, and so each morning before class we would go on a five-mile run, from our hotel up to the castle at the top of the hill. She put me through my paces. What a woman!

I coupled up with Natasha when we were conducting a Feng Shui case study day on a property in Leicester City. Natasha and I were given the task of healing any Geopathic Stress. We discovered a strong line going through the client's bed and we knew that the client had suffered cancer in the past. We worked together well and used a flower offering, earth acupuncture, and divined the animal card of the Deer to support us in our healing ceremony.

Following our course, Olga invited Natasha and I down to her home in Devon. We had been chatting and dreaming of how we wanted to touch the lives of everyone in the UK with Feng

Shui to bring health, harmony, and happiness to our nation. In early October 2011 we gathered in Olga's cuddly, love-filled home and felt blessed to be sharing precious time together.

Earlier that year Olga had lost the love of her life, Karen, to cancer. Olga took us on an adventure to the town of Boscastle, famous for its museum of witchcraft. Whilst in Boscastle we sat outside a café. Natasha and I sat at one side of the table, and Olga sat at the other. Natasha and I had a present for Olga which was a beautiful green malachite heart. Natasha and I put the crystal heart between our hands and injected it with love before we presented it to Olga. As we passed it to Olga with our love and opened our hands to reveal the sacred rock a green dragonfly landed on the empty table setting next to her. A beautiful blissful silence surrounded us; we felt a presence of divine love with us.

Chapter 4: Erotic Dreams

We sat in silence – all connected with ethereal presence. Following the silence and as the dragonfly flew away Olga said that the dragonfly represented the spirit of Karen, her beloved, and that Karen had sent a symbol of herself to bring love into our presence. That was a profound and beautiful experience that will stay with me for the rest of my life. Bless you Karen for blessing us with your presence. Staying with Olga was like a breath of fresh air for me, we lived on the same planet, and we loved to do similar things.

Natasha, Olga, and I divined cards to give us clear messages of our life's journey. During one divining session we decided to divine a card for the three of us – just one card - we used the 'Power Animal Oracle Cards' by Steven D. Farmer Ph.D. Together we selected the Porcupine Card and our message on the card said:

Free Yourself of Guilt and Shame. See the world through the eyes of a child, trusting your inner mother and father to be there whenever you need them. Protection is available when you need it, so you can feel safe in expressing yourself in all the different ways you've always wanted to. There's boldness in innocence, and there's no more need to hide behind any childhood guilt about perceived misdeeds or be consumed with shame about revealing your true self. You're a gentle soul and have never intentionally harmed anyone. Release any guilt over your behaviour or shame about yourself in this situation. There's no need to feel resentful, victimised, or arrogant toward anyone else either. Be the child of God that you are. In your heart, live in the garden. Others may cause you to prickle, but truly, most of what they do or say to you is harmless and not a threat. So be joyful and grateful and let everything you do be done with complete abandon. Dance, laugh, sing, and be free again, just like you were on the day you were born.'

BELIEVE IN LOVE

At the time, Olga, Natasha, and I thought it was a message for us to join and use it in the marketing of our offerings of Feng Shui. Free Yourself. Be Happy. Be Healthy.

We were wrong. This message was a deep message to all of us individually to free ourselves of emotional conditioning, to free ourselves of any self-critical energy. What a powerful message – free yourself.

I think this is a huge message to all of humanity. Release any emotional baggage that is causing you pain, grief, and trauma.

I said farewell to Olga and Natasha on the 5th of October and driving home I could not pass the Glastonbury junction of the M5. I had a massive urge to go and spend a couple of nights alone in this sacred town in Somerset. Glastonbury is said to be the Heart Chakra of the World. I found a great bed and breakfast called Parsnips, which luckily had a room to accommodate me. It was situated at the base of Glastonbury Tor and very close to the Chalice Well Gardens.

The following day I ascended Glastonbury Tor equipped with a pen, my journal, and my dowsing rods. I dowsed and

Chapter 4: Erotic Dreams

detected 8 converging ley lines on the top of the Tor. And as I sat on the positive energy, I allowed myself to dream and to write my Love Wishes and here's an extract of what I wrote in my journal, '***My Specification to Attract my Soul mate. I need, I want, I desire a soul mate to harmonise, to love, to follow a tantric path to heaven. I need to connect with a man who has a spiritual and sexually adventurous spirit like me. A man who will talk to trees, connect with the earth and help heal humanity with me. One day, this lover, friend, playmate, soul mate will come. I glow with love now and forever. I am fulfilled and content.***'

After leaving my husband my relationships had been in turmoil and I felt ready to find the man of my dreams. I knew that to bring about the relationship I wanted would mean creating a clear specification of the soul mate I was to attract.

Following this entry into my journal, saying my prayers, and sending gratitude to my family, friends and to humanity I descended the Tor and spent some quiet time at the Chalice Well Garden sitting in the Angel Chair where I lit candles for my family and friends.

I descended into the town of Glastonbury and spent a few silent hours in the Goddess Temple and read the information about the Goddess Brigit who helps us connect with the fire of life. The fire of passion in our hearts.

Oh, la la. Leaving the Goddess Temple, I felt enriched and full of love. It seemed I had got in touch with my goddess inside. As I strolled back to Parsnips through the main street, I saw a shop called Enlightenment that specialized in artisan crafts from Nepal. I was drawn into the beautiful shop and bought an abundance of amazing items for my home including erotic books, sculptures, and a brass gong to cleanse my house.

But my most significant purchase was an erotic painting of a beautiful male angel swooping down to earth holding a woman and caressing her naked breast.

Eros and Psyche

This picture was of a sculpture titled 'Eros and Psyche' by Antonio Canova. I only recently found this out and discovered that Eros was not born of an individual but was one of the primordial forces. Eros is the embodiment of amorous passion and an erotic protector. Eros is the protector of men and of women and also the protector of relationships between men and women. Eros depicts the passion of erotic enjoyment, the need for delight and spiritual nourishment.

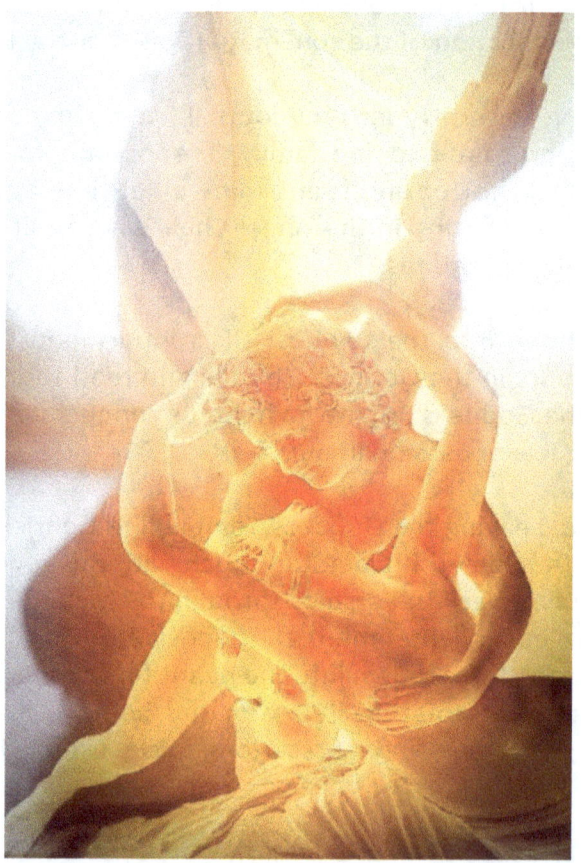

Chapter 4: Erotic Dreams

This picture helped me manifest my Eros, my sex god, my soul mate, my kindred spirit, my twin flame. My ultimate partner, my forever man.

It's because of that simple purchase that we decided to call this book BELIEVE IN LOVE as it is this picture that made all my love wishes come true. We considered calling the book 'Find Your Eros' or 'Find Your Sex God' as this is what I was dreaming of at the time I walked into that shop. I was dreaming of a spiritually and sexually blissful relationship, allowing me to experience tantric bliss or relationship bliss.

When I arrived back in my room at Parsnips, I decided to dowse my bedroom to see if any of the sacred ley lines passed through my room as I was staying so close to the sacred sites of Chalice Well and Glastonbury Tor.
To my surprise, I had a ley line running through my bed. Oh wow, I had slept and was sleeping on a sacred energy line!

Nanu Nanu – The Connection

The most beautiful event followed. A text conversation that changed the course of my life.

I received a text from Lionel. Remember, he was the gentleman I'd met at the Manchester University Leadership Masterclass and agreed to do a talk for his charity.

I sent back a response. I was excited to tell Lionel about how I was sleeping on an auspicious positive energy line. A ley line. His response was, 'you will probably have **erotic dreams'**. Well, that was it for me. I thought back to when I met him and remembered that he had great hair, a nice bum, he was tall and attractive, and he talked tantra.

BELIEVE IN LOVE

So, at 6pm on the 6th of October 2011 the erotic texts started – around 800 of them were sent back and forth in two weeks. Okay in truth, they were not exactly texts, they were sexts.

We did not know each other. We were both free creative spirits and so what followed was pure creative fantasy. We could be whoever we wanted to be. Our spirits danced in the ether together. Following two weeks of blissful connection with texts, we decided to talk. We pronounced our time to connect verbally as the love hour, we decided on 2pm on 22nd October.

I believe it was me putting my clear intentions and specification through the ley lines that brought Lionel and I together. The ley line I was sleeping on went through Parsnips, through Glastonbury Tor and then up to the Northwest of England where Lionel lived.

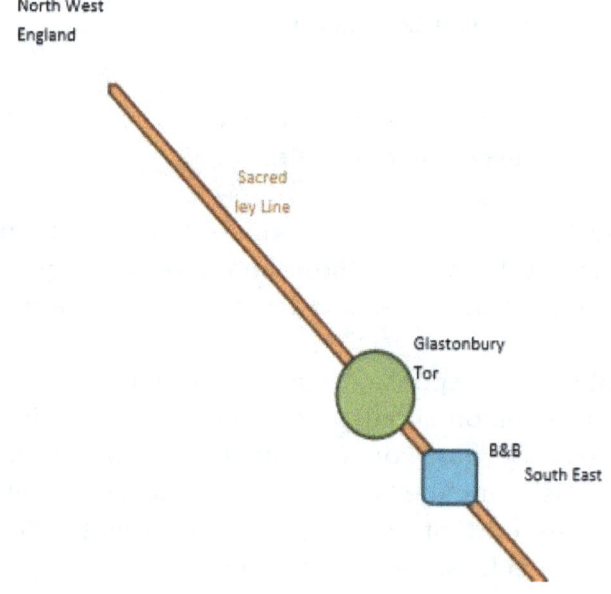

Chapter 4: Erotic Dreams

Just before I leave this Erotic Dreams chapter, I want to enlighten you with the five languages of love. Lionel and I discovered the Five Love Languages by Gary Chapman later in our relationship. It confirmed our similarity in the way we express heartfelt commitment to each other. Our top languages, meaning the way we best excite each other, through words of affirmation, touch and quality time are virtually equal for both of us.

Being specific in your requirements is the first part to manifesting the love of your life. Unless you take the time to consider and write out your love wishes and what you want in another person, you're playing a hit and miss game with who and what you'll get.

A vision board can give us a subconscious boost every time we look at it, or a conscious understanding each time we study what we've put on it. Doing the same for a partner can be a creative way to find the right person for you.

So few people actually take the time to focus on what they want. Think of it on an emotional and spiritual level as well as the physical level. Most current relationships seem to have been guided purely by the first flush of attraction. Whilst this may work for short term relationships, if you want a partner that will take you to another level of physical joy, it won't be just physical play that will get you there. Being able and willing to talk about anything and being able to find balance in spiritual harmony will far outlive anything you can have on an initial physical basis.

So, Lionel's long descriptive texts full of stories, poems and inspirational words resonated with me at a deep level. I believe we fell in love in the ether before we even had our first date. I later found out that Lionel too had written his love wishes down, a clear specification for the woman of his dreams.

This note had been hidden away for some time. Part if it read: *'A fun and exciting ginger haired woman with succulent breasts and a great appetite for sex. Equal social standing, independent, intelligent, and intriguing.'* Sums me up perfectly!

Chapter 5
The Shock

Oh, la la. The time had arrived to talk to this very sexy man in person. How excited was I? As a man he fitted my specification of a soul mate to a tee.

Our verbal connection was booked for 2pm on the 22nd of October 2011, just two weeks two days after we had romantically connected through the ley lines. I had been in fantasy paradise for the whole two weeks since we connected, I was obsessed, possessed by this gorgeous man with long golden curly hair, the Lion Man.

As I mentioned in Chapter 4, our top love language is words of affirmation. I had received thousands of words texted to me from Lionel in those two weeks. Lionel had aroused my lioness instincts and wow was I ready, really ready to connect with this man. In my Feng Shui world, the number two is the symbol of love and so we would have our first conversation on the phone at 2pm on the 22nd. I prepared myself for this momentous occasion.

I prepared a beautiful altar with a Balinese style offering. I placed my beautiful Balinese altar cloth on the altar table and placed on it symbols of love. Along with my Balinese temple bells, I lit my special sacred incense and set the scene. I placed my yin yang dedication cushion in front of the altar, and I sat and meditated and sent love to my family, friends, and the world, giving gratitude for my life. I sent love to Lionel in the ether, praying that our verbal connection would lead to a physical connection - to love, lust and a blissful relationship.

BELIEVE IN LOVE

I rang my Balinese temple bells – one male bell and one female bell to harmonise the space. I filled my living room with love. I was ready.

I was so nervous. I was so excited. I was elated. I had butterflies fluttering in my tummy. I was about to talk to this beautiful poetic man – the man who had seduced me with his words.

I called his number and took some deep breaths to calm my nerves. Lionel answered, "Hello, Lionel speaking". I purred like a lioness as I spoke in awe of this king of the jungle. Before I could say very much, Lionel interrupted me and said, "Dawn, it is very important that I share something with you first."

Wait for it. Here it comes. Here comes the shock. "I'm currently having relationships with six women."

This was a massive shock to me. Wow. I said to Lionel after catching my breath, "OK I just need to think about this and call you back." My thoughts were pinging round my head trying to evaluate the situation. What questions did I need to ask? This guy must be the most amazing lover on this planet. Mmmm yum yum!

Yes, I was in shock, but my thoughts quickly put some questions in my mind to ask Lionel. I wanted to know if he had had long-term relationships with these ladies. This would mean that he was not sleeping around with a lot of different women. This may be ok.

I called him back and I had my questions answered. It's not what you are thinking - he was not a promiscuous man sleeping with many different women at once. I may have set the wrong scene. Lionel was having long term relationships with these six women, including tantric/sexual relations.

Chapter 5: The Shock

I decided that I would be number seven.

Well, why not. I absolutely love sex and I remembered talking to Lionel about tantra within the first five minutes of meeting him. That excited me, a man who was mystical and adventurous. I had decided that I was ready for passion as Lionel's texts had sent me into a frenzy. I was so worried I might seduce him in the first hour of meeting.

Since separating from my husband, I had made a pact with myself. There were four rules I would stick to:

1. I was never getting married again
2. I was never going to live with a man again
3. I was ready for adventure
4. I was ready for adventurous sex

I was really ready for 3 and 4!

I wanted to connect with this spiritual Lion Man who had turned me on so much in his texts. I called Lionel back at 2.22 pm. Before long our first date was set.

The other thing we spoke about when we first met at the University was Feng Shui, so I suggested that our first date was to be a sniffing date. We agreed to have a date for each of our senses. Smell, sight, sound, taste then touch.

Oh, la la! Again, I was so excited. The sniffing date was set for 7pm on 26th October 2011 at a pub in Manchester, UK.

What do I wear? What colour, what texture? Will I look sexy enough? I contemplated the date deeply and yes, I was excited but also, I had a deep spiritual yearning, a voice inside me told me to start this date as I meant to go on. So, I got a copy of **Deepak Chopra's book, 'The Seven Spiritual Laws of Success '**.

The Seven Spiritual Laws of Success are: -
1. The law of pure potentiality
2. The law of giving
3. The law of Karma or cause and effect
4. The law of least effort
5. The law of intention and desire
6. The law of detachment
7. The law of Dharma or purpose in life.

Oh, how I love this book.

I really recommend you read it. It really gives you an insight to bring balance and harmony into your life. It brings you a feeling of inner peace. It brings you an inner knowing of wholeness and freedom of spirit. It brings you a feeling of love and completeness. It brings you hope.

OK, I have my book packed. I've got my bright orange jumper on (orange is my signature colour). I arrived early - those who know me will be saying, 'Wow Dawn, this was the first time ever'.

I entered the large roomy pub and ordered my usual pint of warm water with a slice of lemon and wandered around to find Lionel. He was nowhere to be seen. I found a look-out seat so that I could view the entrance, I planned to pounce on him as soon as he arrived. Ten minutes went by. No Lionel.

My phone bleeped telling me I had a text message. It was Lionel apologizing that he would be about an hour late. Boy, was I glad I had that book with me? I began to read it's wondrous words while waiting. For such a powerful book, it is only short and takes just one hour to read. This would fill my time perfectly. By the time Lionel arrived, I had read the book cover to cover.

Chapter 5: The Shock

When I recall this story to other women, they tell me that they wouldn't have waited, but I had a deep inner voice of calm which spoke to me that night telling me to stay. That inner passion in you, that deep inner voice of calm is your intuition, you need to listen to it. Your intuition is your true self, it is your inner child. Learn to let it flow through you naturally.

Oh, my goodness, I spotted Lionel arriving and rushed over to him. It was then I remembered we were having a sniffing date, so I slowed down, and we approached each other at snail's pace. We started slowly, looking into each other's eyes. Wow! was this man attractive.

Lionel's tall and gorgeous physique looked good in his business suit. And I loved his long golden curly hair. We murmured hello gently. We tenderly held out our arms to hold each other and embrace. Being close we could glide our nostrils over each other's faces and necks to investigate our aromas. Thinking back, I can remember smiling, not just with my mouth and face, but with my whole body too. I was so incredibly happy. I could see Lionel was too.

We decided to eat and proceeded upstairs to find somewhere comfy to sit. Our attraction was instant, but kissing was not allowed, just sniffing, so that is just what we did. What a turn on.

Lionel asked me back to his place after we'd eaten, and I said yes quickly. We walked outside into the fresh night air, we both looked up to see the sparkling stars above us, then looked at each other and POW - we had our first kiss. It was delicious.

We continued with much more than kisses back at Lionel's home.

The Feng Shui dates we planned to have, where we indulged

in just one of our senses at a time, were overtaken by passion.

Chapter 6
Tantric Bliss

On the 1st of November 2011 (1.11.11) our third date, I stayed over at Lionel's place. We indulged in all our senses that evening. We melted into each other's essence, made love, and lay in bed chatting and laughing. What happened to me next was life changing. Playfully I'd positioned myself with my legs either side of Lionel's chest. I didn't know it at the time, but I'd placed my Base Chakra on top of Lionel's Heart Chakra. Out of nowhere I had the most explosive inner orgasmic eruption that vibrated my whole-body, I felt it from the base of my spine to the top of my head. This pure bliss continued for around half an hour. Wow!

I had briefly experienced a similar feeling in Bali at the Kundalini Tantra Ashram, dancing around a Shiva Lingam with one hundred Balinese men and women. I was mystified and asked Lionel what he had done to me. How did he do that?

Lionel had placed a special hand mudra on an area he called my Muladhara (near the coccyx at the base of the spine. He had activated my Kundalini (spiritual energy) to rise and rise and keep on rising to take me to an ecstatic state. I became obsessed with this incredible magical mystical man. How had he learnt this technique? Did it happen with all his women? Lionel explained to me he could sense my high vibrational energy the day we met. He said that we were vibrating at a similar frequency and open to experiencing divine energy together.

Boy, I had so much to learn from this man; I had a lot to learn about myself. I had lots of fun and incredible experiences as over the following weeks Lionel taught me about the seven chakras and the spiritual power flowing within our bodies.

BELIEVE IN LOVE

Lionel has been meditating and opening his chakras since the age of 14. Lionel rises at 4.32am each morning and spends two hours or more in a spiritual practice every day called Mae Li. This apparently means the flow of life. He uses one special hand mudra which is placed in differing positions on each chakra. Lionel is a Master of this technique and willingly shares his knowledge with others to discover this divine ritual to harmonize body, mind, and spirit. *(Lionel teaches more about chakras in Part 3.)*

I also believe that this feeling of bliss was made possible because of my spiritual practice that I discovered in Bali, and my practical daily life of giving gratitude to my family, the sun, nature spirits and the Universe which had opened me up to connect with Lionel's pure energy. I further believe, it was the divine essence within each of us that was connecting and reacting and creating tantric bliss for us.

I now understood this energy. I call tantra a 'ménage à trois' with the divine.

From that day forward Lionel and I continue to have the most beautiful tantric vibrational relationship. Neither of us had experienced such energy before. Each time we came together, and we were in a calm connected state, or on sacred land I would spontaneously orgasm and erupt inside. This would happen in shops, in the car, on trains, on planes. I felt as if I had fallen in love with an extra-terrestrial being with special powers.

Prior to meeting Lionel, I had created a Tantra Temple at my home. In the dome was a four-metre diameter bed dressed in satin sheets and gorgeous drapes. The colours I chose for my dome were chakra colours. It was if I had a premonition that I was going to meet this Master of Tantra and had prepared a space for our intimate connection.

Chapter 6: Tantric Bliss

The bed was the perfect size for us to lie head-to-head, Crown Chakra to Crown Chakra, invoking our ecstatic state and simply being in Tantric Bliss without even touching each other.

Chapter 7
The Hanky Panky Pond

In December 2011, I decided to invite Flying Star Feng Shui Master, Richard Ashworth, to do an in-depth survey of my home and help me place auspicious rocks around the site to enhance the positive Feng Shui. Richard arrived and used his Luo Pan Compass to check all the directions and flying star calculations. That night Richard stayed over to update me on his findings.

We sat in front of a big roaring fire that evening, Richard asked me what had happened in my life since I'd installed the new pond. I explained to him that a new man had entered my life and our relationship was physically, emotionally, and spiritually amazing. Richard insisted that by installing the pond in the position I had, I had changed the whole energy of the property and he announced that my pond was a Hanky Panky pond. He looked up at my fireplace and saw the word **EROS** sculptured in the wood, he pointed the word out to me and said, **"Eros, that means erotic love"**. Everything connected.

Richard asked me the date the Hanky Panky pond was filled with water. It was the 6th of October 2011, the date when I was in Glastonbury and the date when I manifested the man of my dreams. Just wow!

So, in my belief system, the Hanky Panky pond at Heather Bank Farm acted like an earth acupressure point to ignite the flow of connection through the natural web of ley lines which connected Lionel and me. That, and a combination of my clear intentions, along with the erotic picture I purchased made all the difference. I studied the picture of the Angel (Eros) landing on earth seducing the beautiful woman (Psyche) and to my amazement the male angel 'Eros' resembled Lionel. The same bone structure and the same long curly hair. I'd found my Eros.

Hanky Panky dates with Lionel were amazing. He excited me, he thrilled me, he filled me with so much passion like no other man in my life had ever been able to do. We had spiritual dates too where we would go to meditations and talks at the Brahma Kumaris Centre in Manchester. We had a spiritual date at the Gorton Monastery Manchester on 11.11.11. It was pure Bliss.

Many amazing dates followed. It was clear what attracted me to Lionel. Lionel was attracted to me because of my passion, my energy, my connection to Feng Shui and my spirituality. Our favourite time was a month-long date in Bali, the time together was simply blissful. We spent time at the Bali Spirit Festival and then stayed on for the Island Space Clearing Festival. Lionel and I had such fun dancing in the streets of a Balinese village with the Giant Ogoh Ogoh monsters cleansing the negative energy out of Bali.

While we were there, we experienced Nyepi Day, a day of pure silence. No one was allowed out on the streets, and no one was allowed to speak. Lionel and I respected this tradition and stayed in silence for 24 hours. Instead, we communicated through our eyes, lips, limbs, and body language. It was intense and beautiful.

It will come as no surprise that we have spent many romantic nights together but one of the most amazing nights of my life was with Lionel in April 2013 at a resort in Ubud Bali called the Five Elements.

You could feel the auspicious energy of the Ayung River wave its way around the resort. The night we stayed there was a fire ceremony with around six Balinese priests chanting and ringing Balinese temple bells. The ritual involved us all smashing a coconut shell into a fire – the shell represented our ego which

Chapter 7: The Hanky Panky Pond

we were letting go of.

After the ceremony, we were covered in flower petals and the Balinese priest tied a Hindu black, white and red bracelet onto our wrists. The three colours represent the three Hindu gods: Brahma, Vishnu, and Shiva.

To Lionel and I the colours represented the trilogy which we believed in: Physical, Emotional and Spiritual harmony.

Chapter 8
Heaven's Edge

For six months, I experienced heaven on earth with Lionel. I was obsessed with him. He excited me so much I could not get enough of him. I concluded that this was not healthy for me. I had an attachment to him and was pre-occupied with sex and tantra. My friends were getting fed up with me. All I spoke about was Lionel, sex, sex, and more sex.

Remember the pact I made to myself when I was 50? The deal I made stating that I would never live with another man or remarry after I split up from my husband? It's for these reasons that I ended my relationship with Lionel in **April 2012.**

Lionel confidently said to me that I would be back as he believed us to be soul mates, I wouldn't accept that.

Just one month after ending our relationship, I again attended Tony Robbins' conference, 'Unleash the Power Within' in London where I first learned to 'fire walk'. I knew Lionel would be there. During the event Tony asked us, the delegates, to close our eyes and reach out for the people who you love and who make you feel good. Lionel kept popping into my mind.

So, I text Lionel. He was at the back of the 8000-strong room at the Excel Centre, and I was at the front.

I will never ever forget this moment. I sent another text and asked if we could meet for a last kiss.

We had that kiss. As we walked towards each other it was like the parting of the Red Sea as the crowds of people opened up for us. The eye contact, the body language, the pure beauty of this sexually provocative man set my senses on fire. The kiss was electric. Wow!

Just before we parted Lionel whispered in my ear, "Dawny, will you come to Fiji with me and be with me on 12.12.12?" Tony Robbins had explained that he believed Fiji was the happiest place on the planet. Lionel had taken inspiration from this and decided that he wanted to be with his soul mate on this auspicious day in a very special place on earth.

I said no.

In June 2012, two months after our breakup we met up. I wanted to give Lionel the picture of the Erotic Angels that had manifested him in the first place. On the back of this picture, I wrote:

'To Lionel. The awakening twin flames burn as one for eternity. I give you this to bring a sacred union into your life. Yes, we are a sacred union of twin souls/twin flames, we reflect each other. We are destined to do something special together on this planet. High Priest and High Priestess. Given with love. Offering for today 30th June 2012. Want what you have and don't want what you don't have. Dawny Bird'

I always had a vision of Lionel and I being High Priest and High Priestess and I could see us both dressed in white robes hosting ceremonies together, but I could not see us as a couple. I passed the picture to Lionel and said farewell. We had a last kiss beneath an umbrella in the rain as we parted.

Oh, my goodness, it was so hard to say goodbye. I wanted to seduce him there and then in the park, but I resisted. I knew that saying goodbye was for best for both of us.

Chapter 8: Heavens Edge

In August that year I went on a spiritual retreat to sort my emotional state out. I had concluded that I needed to get in touch with my feminine side, my yin. All my life, I had been a yang courageous creative colourful woman. When I thought back to all the men I had dated in my life, it occurred to me that not one of them had ever asked me out on a date. I was always the instigator.

I was a woman who asked and got what she wanted. I was in a state of flux, in a state of confusion. Lionel was the first to ask me; he could see we were perfect for each other. He could see something that I could not. So, I needed to work on me, I needed to rebalance.

First, I had some therapy with a lovely friend called Reverend Alison Levesley who put me through a visualization exercise. She helped me look within me, at my inner masculine and feminine side. Looking at the imbalance within me was scary.

In a hypnotic trance state, she took me to my yang masculine side. I was in heaven. It was hot and passionate. I could see orange and red flames of desire and beauty. But then she took me into my feminine yin side. *Aaarrrhhhhh*! Get me out of this place. It was ice cold, full of icicles that were falling and stabbing me. Alison guided me to a middle ground and helped me melt the icicles and merge the cold yin with the hot passionate yang and transform my inner self into a beautiful rainbow.

When I awoke from the therapeutic encounter, I felt elated.

The second thing I did was to go to a Buddhist retreat following a suggestion from my older daughter who had just been there alone and returned home feeling incredibly inspired. This was a great idea, so I invited my younger daughter to accompany me to Koh Samui in Thailand in August 2012 where this time I indulged in the mind and emotional detox programme.

The mind, body and spiritual cleansing at the Kamalaya Wellness Resort brought about some major realizations of who I was. I realized all the conditioning connected to my parents and their influence on me. I rang Lionel several times from the retreat, I needed to hear his voice and tell him what I was doing. I returned home a more balanced and harmonic woman.

At the beginning of September 2012, I received a text from Lionel. He had booked two places on a spiritual weekend in Looe in Cornwall, it was called The Ishaya Ascension weekend. I felt in a good place, I was balanced and together, so I said yes.

We met on the 15th of September at Exeter railway station. Oh my, the sight of Lionel set my heart pounding and our passionate kiss on the car park was commented on by a passer-by; "get a room" he shouted. And do you know what, that's exactly what we did. We made love for the first time in months.

After another magical physical reconnection, we went for a walk. We walked through the streets of Exeter and found a restaurant across from the Cathedral. I felt as if I was in a bubble of bliss sitting next to Lionel and then Lionel asked the question again. "Dawny, will you come to Fiji with me for 12.12.12?" And guess what I said?

Yes, yes, yes!

Lionel jumped up and danced around the restaurant. He shared our news with the waitresses and the other customers. I think he was pleased. I know I was.

We spent an incredible time together at the Ishaya Ascension weekend where we truly connected at a different blissful

Chapter 8: Heavens Edge

spiritual level.

I really must thank, Wendy Windle, whom I've never met. She's an Ishaya Ascensionist Monk, who Lionel met on the London underground, she introduced him to the belief and uplifted his spirits in a time of dire need.

It was now December 2012. We left the cold weather behind us and flew to Fiji. I officially became a member of the Mile-High Club. Wickedly naughty – but oh so wonderful! Once we reached Fiji, Lionel asked me where I would like to spend the special day; the 12th day of the 12th month 2012. I knew exactly what to do, I divined the map of Fiji and her islands to find out the most auspicious energy to help us choose our special place.

We identified two powerful places on the map. One called **'Heaven's Edge'** which was up in the mountains on the Nandi Island around 40 miles in land in the central mountain range. The other was a small island called Matamanoa. We decided to save Matamanoa for the 12$^{th\ of}$ December and to adventure to Heaven's Edge before the auspicious day.

Heaven's Edge was a deserted paradise, a natural utopia, we could see nothing obviously man-made was there. It was quite a journey, but thanks to our trusty jeep and some local tribe intervention we got there. At Heaven's Edge we went for a walk between the volcanic boulders. The energy of the place was amazing, it was secluded, lush and vibrant. While we were there, clouds began to dance above us, and sweet refreshing drops of rain started to fall. The speed of the once gentle drops quickened into a heavy tropical rainstorm, we took off our clothes, our naked flesh was covered in steaming rain drops and the long grass made a magnificent bed to connect us to the Earth. As the storm passed, we lay there savouring the fresh aromas of our bodies and nature all around us. Oh, la la.

Chapter 9
Sexual Transmutation – The Sacred Trilogy

Before flying to the tropical Island of Matamanoa we indulged in love making high on a volcano, experienced naked mud wrestling in the Valley of the Sleeping Giant, bathed together in a bath of coconut milk and we swam naked in fresh mountain waterfalls.

BELIEVE IN LOVE

We were free and liberated. We melted into each other's essence. We were in tantric bliss.

I must share with you something Lionel introduced me to early on in our relationship. Remember that time I kept rejecting him? The time when it seemed obvious that we were deepening in love, but I still wouldn't admit it to myself? Lionel repeatedly asked me to read Chapter 11 of Napoleon Hills' book, 'Think and Grow Rich'. Lionel has been reading this book as his business bible for many years.

On his recommendation I bought the book and saw that Chapter 11 was titled Sexual Transmutation.

Oh my, I thought something weird and kinky was about to be revealed to me, but I was wrong. It taught me about a sacred spiritual connection between two people within a physical relationship. It was about feeling spirit and feeling divinity within your relationship. The Sexual Transmutation was about the harmonization of energy: Physical, Emotional and Spiritual. The sacred trilogy.

Lionel knew all along that we had that sacred trilogy. On the 11th ^{of} December, we flew by helicopter from Nandi to Matamanoa. Wow! it was stunning. When we landed, we were greeted with a Fijian welcome, there was music and garlands of shells were laced around our necks.

From early in our relationship, we had named each other the Lion Man and the Dawny Bird. These pet-names suited our characters exactly. Our room at this resort was Hut One and as we walked through our door we were dumbfounded. All over the ceiling were ancient drawings of lions and birds. This was a clear message from the Universe, or the Divine Source as we now know it to be. Even though there were twelve huts on the island, only our hut was decorated in this way.

Chapter 9: Sexual Transmutation – The Sacred Trilogy

The 12th day of the 12th month finally arrived, and we started our journey to the highest point of Matamanoa. We were the only people there, we were completely alone, but there was evidence of much love and joy as visitors before us had left mementoes of their love on a single bush. As we checked for the auspicious time of 12.12pm, we looked around from this vantage point at the world of incredible beauty before us. Lionel held my hands, looked deep into my eyes and my soul, and asked me if I would share the rest of my life with him. He said this with such love and passion from deep within his heart. He produced a little box that he'd carefully hidden in his shorts which held inside a beautiful golden ring with a single pearl mounted on it. I said YES without hesitation. The pearl signifies wisdom through experience and amazingly one of my psychic friends had previously told me I would be proposed to on a mountain with a pearl ring. A pure wow factor moment.

You can imagine what happened next. Yep, you guessed it, tears of joy poured down my cheeks. Lionel put the pearl ring on my finger. The intimacy, the bliss, the sacredness of the rest of our time in Fiji went into oblivion. I was the happiest, most fulfilled woman on this planet.

The beauty of our relationship is that our love is unconditional; we are free spirits choosing to be together, choosing to stay

Chapter 9: Sexual Transmutation – The Sacred Trilogy

together and live in blissful harmony.

Conclusion:

Thank you, ley lines,
Thank you, Eros and Psyche, Thank you, Feng Shui, Thank you, Tantra,
Thank you, Sacred Divine Energy, for bringing our souls together to live in Bliss

Review of Part 1 of This Book by Rev. Deana Stone-Pierce.

"This beautifully written story will take you on a journey back to peace, to harmony, to deep inner joy, to love and to the Divine.

Dawn dares to challenge the status quo and experiences living from her source, acting with positive and creative energy to make her desires real, contrary to all the scepticism from her business associates, friends, family, and community.

This story will give you the opportunity to discover some

ancient past processes and explore some of the greatest mysteries of our time. Through understanding the developments, it will be revealed how it is possible to change negative into positive, the undesirable into desirable and failure into success. All which is completely demonstrated throughout this book.

Dawn reveals her new-found skills and knowledge of how to replace thoughts of despair, limitations, unhappiness, and failure with thoughts of hope, courage, abundance, and new possibilities.

As these take root in thought process, bodily cells are transformed. You can begin to see life in a whole new way. The old fades away while new things in harmonious vibration to your thoughts can take place. Your bodily cells that were comprised of negative thoughts can be exchanged with thoughts of higher vibrational positive energy. Life can have a new meaning. Your heart can be filled with peace, hope, joy, vigour, and a new-found confidence.

This book pinpoints the simple act that change can be made not only through the physical body, emotions, and perspective, but your conditioning, relationships and surroundings can also alter.

Through your understanding it is hoped that you gain self-acceptance and that you are now at the dawn of a new beginning in your life. A life which is full of boundless opportunities. Anyone who is able to fully understand this creative knowledge presented in this book will have the ability to transform their life into whatsoever they desire. Knowledge is power. Spiritual creative knowledge is unlimited power.

I have personally experienced these sorts of changes in the reading of this book that you now hold in your hands.

Chapter 9: Sexual Transmutation – The Sacred Trilogy

Even when sceptical your inner beliefs can always work. Faith is found in the newly established skills which are recognised and connected with the inner knowing. Awakening to inner faith (self-confidence) is something totally real and is to be found at inner levels of one's being. (Faith is not external but internal to each and every one of us). It is a gift given to us by our creator (Divine) together with the gift of life itself.

Faith (inner knowing) is an energy that is natural to us and that we can sooner rather than later work within its positive and creative form, especially for our inner growth. What is Faith? "A belief based on unknown testimony" (taken from the illustrated dictionary). The Apostle Paul defines it as: "The firm security of what we hope for, the conviction of what we do not see" (Hebrews 11.1). An active energy that moves either positively or negatively, according to the decision that is driving us.

Beautiful Dawn's appreciation for her innovative gifts and for her totally accepting inner knowing uncovers great opulence through all that naturally flows. Trusting and broadening her knowledge uniquely, serving her family, friends, home, business, and community with LOVE!

This story will help you see opportunities and possibilities that before had gone unnoticed. The spiritual energy of Dawn's success and beliefs throughout fills and radiates all around you drawing you to individuals and circumstances that can help you to achieve the success you desire and in turn can change your environment and conditions."

Namaste.
Enjoy your Journey of Growth. Rev. Deana Stone-Pearce

STEP 2: DISCOVER:
Practices to Discover Inner Happiness and Awaken Your Hidden Powers by Lionel and Dawn

STEP 2 of our book is for you to discover inner happiness by awakening your hidden powers. You may not believe you have any, but in our eyes, you do. We all do.

Our journey has taken many routes and we have invested a lot of time and money in self-discovery and personal development. In the pages that follow we invite you to learn some of the practices we've used and still do, to bring balance to our trilogy: our physical, emotional, and spiritual self.

The following pages invite you to discover and to learn the practices which have opened us to experience deep inner happiness.

Enjoy your journey to ecstatic bliss. Be happy. Wake happy. Sleep happy. Eat happy. Think happy. Live happy.

Dedication

Chapter 1 - How to use Divining Cards for Inner Happiness

Chapter 2 - How to use Divining Rods

Chapter 3 - How to use a Divining Pendulum Chapter 4 - How to Divine with Your Body

Chapter 5 - How to Discover Your Purpose, Passion, & Power.

Chapter 6 - How to Live in a Healthy Home

Chapter 7 - How to Live in a Happy Home

Chapter 8 - How to Create the Life of Your Dreams

Chapter 9 - How to be a Pearl Fisher

Chapter 10 - How to Calm Your Mind with Mantras

Chapter 11 - How to Nourish Your Soul with Chanting.

Chapter 12 - How to Connect with Nature

Chapter 13 - How to Experience Tantra

Chapter 14 - How to Nurture Your Spirit

Chapter 15 - How to Transform Darkness to Light

Chapter 16 - How to Find Your Soul Tribe

Chapter 17 - How to Balance Your Mind, Body, and Soul with Ayurveda

Dedication

Step 2 of this book 'Discover' is dedicated to the late, great Rob Gray who introduced Dawn to unseen energy and helped her discover her hidden powers. Rob Gray founded and was principal teacher at the Feng Shui Academy. Rob inspired Dawn in so many ways, his teaching style, his vast knowledge of Feng Shui, his authenticity, his love affair with Carolina his soul mate and wife, his dedication as a father to Christian.

STEP 2 – Discover is Created in Memory of Robert Gray.

Here is Rob's purpose transcended from 'I' to 'we' and 'my' to 'our' with the permission of Carolina Gray, 9th July 2015.

We, Rob's students have permission to use Rob's purpose to continue his work and bless this planet with his spirit.

Our purpose

We commit to be the most positive, progressive, and loving force in the lives of others we can possibly be.

Our purpose is to extinguish fear and negativity by empowering and radiating love, happiness, and unity always, with honesty and integrity.

BELIEVE IN LOVE

We commit to offer any help, advice and knowledge to others that aid their purpose, help them to own their own lives and accelerate their evolution, and help them to be happier, more loved, and more loving. We do this by our own example, through advice, listening and touching souls with our love and warmth. By enlivening bliss and bringing about love in this way we can remove people's conditioned boundaries of restriction and put them in touch with the field of all possibilities. In the never-ending and passionate pursuit of this purpose, everything we sow, we say, and we think is in complete alignment with it and therefore we are constantly growing and evolving, raising cosmic consciousness simultaneously and benefiting all.

Chapter 1
How to Divine with Cards to Discover Inner Happiness

I would say that this is one of my favourite pastimes and the inspiration for my life's direction. I am specifically talking about Divination Cards sometimes referred to as Oracle Cards. They are a pack of cards with deep inspirational messages on. I think the first Divining Cards I ever purchased were Animal Spirit cards. Wow, did I get a lot of use out of these cards, they helped me make so many decisions in my life.

Whilst out in Bali in 2014 my deliciously creative soul mate Lionel wrote a set of Divination Cards. We were staying at the Ubud Village Hotel in Nyuh Kuning. It was a hotel where every bedroom had a mini outdoor swimming pool. So, we freed ourselves of clothes and spent most of the time naked whist in our room and in our private garden area. Lionel's creativity just flowed and produced 69 Divination Cards he called Love Wisdom cards. Lionel wrote the beautiful messages, and I designed them – we had a couple of sets printed and have used them so many times in our workshops and seminars.

On the back of the cards, we put the 'manifestation' angel EROS together with Lionel's writing, and on the front just a simple image using cerise pink one of the colours found in the heart chakra. These cards are powerful, they reveal just what we need to focus on.

So, how do you divine with a card deck?

Dependent on which divination cards you are using please read the instructions and do as the author of the cards guides you, or you can do what we like to do and just go for it!

BELIEVE IN LOVE

I put the card deck on my heart and ask for their guidance. I then shuffle them and **ask a clear question**, never a question needing a yes or no answer, always a question where you need guidance. You can ask anything, such as:

How can I become healthier/happier? What do I need to find true love?
What do I need to discover my soul mate?

Be creative and very clear with your questions and repeat it over and over as you connect and shuffle the cards. When you feel satisfied your question is within the card deck – spread the cards out, with the message side face down.

Either stand back or view the cards, scanning them until you see just one that attracts you. Or sensitize your hands by rubbing them together or blowing on them and then with the hand of your choice gently hover your palm over the pack of cards and move it across the cards slowly. You will find that some of the cards make your hand or fingers tingle.

If you feel numerous cards making your hand or fingers tingle remove them from the pack and lay them out next to each other away from the cards that you did not connect with. Continue this process until you find the one you have the strongest connection to. Do not allow yourself to be distracted, be present and turn over the strongest card to reveal your message. Read and absorb the message. Remember to enjoy this feeling too.

To me this is a way to gain direct messages from the Divine source of love, helping us on our journey in life.

Bless all the authors of Divination Cards for bringing such guidance and beauty into our lives.

Chapter 1: How to Divine with Cards to Discover Inner Happiness

We now have around 50 packs of various cards and our current favourite are by a lady called Alana Fairchild. She has channelled numerous decks of cards and aligns them with the most talented artists to beautifully illustrate the card's messages. My favourites are:

Kuan Yin in Oracle Sacred Rebel Oracle Light Workers' Oracle

I also love the cards with a connection to healing. In the healing process Alana asks you to close your eyes as she takes you through a visualization process followed by a prayer. This can be tricky to do when you are reading the message, so, I record the reading on my phone and play it back numerous times to help the healing connect to my mind, body, and soul.

My first card experience with the Animal Spirit oracle was profound. I was staying with my friends Olga and Natasha, and we decided to ask the Animal Spirit Cards collectively what we needed to nourish our lives and move on to a life of health, happiness, and bliss. We took turns to shuffle the cards and as we did, we injected our energy and question into the cards.

We all chose one card individually and did not look at them. We placed our individual cards face down in the centre. Using only our hands we sensed which card from the three was for us all and we all chose the same one. The Porcupine 'Free Yourself'. This has been the most profound card of my life.

'Free Yourself of Innocence. Free Yourself of Guilt and Shame. See the world through the eyes of a child, trusting your inner mother and father to be there whenever you need them. Protection is available when you need it, so you can feel safe in expressing yourself in all the different ways you've always wanted to. There's boldness in innocence, and there's no more need to hide behind any childhood guilt about perceived misdeeds or be consumed with shame about revealing your true self. You're a gentle soul

and have never intentionally harmed anyone. Release any guilt over your behaviour or shame about yourself in this situation. There's no need to feel resentful, victimized, or arrogant toward anyone else either. Be the child of God that you are. In your heart, live in the garden. Others may cause you to prickle, but truly, most of what they do or say to you is harmless and not a threat. So be joyful and grateful and let everything you do be done with complete abandon. Dance, laugh, sing, and be free again, just like you were on the day you were born.'

Chapter 2
How to use Divining Rods

Dowsing and divining have been a part of the skills I have acquired on my journey over the past twenty-five years. Using them is a matter of understanding their value and the energy they carry.

What is Divining? Divining, also called dowsing or radiesthesia, can be used for finding things and answering questions. Everyone can divine. It is a skill that can be honed and perfected. Divining with parallel metal rods (L-rods) uses the movement of the rods to divine an answer.
According to some users of divining rods, brass or copper are good conductors of energy and allow the rod to attune to magnetic fields emanated by the target without the earth's magnetic field interfering. Copper is considered a mineral of energy and mental agility and can aid psychic abilities. Copper is an excellent conductor of energy, from electricity to the mystical subtle energies emanating from higher planes. The handles of the rods are often encased in a material, such as decorative beads, which will allow the L-rods to swing freely, while also providing a constant electrical impedance, to prevent the dowser's own conductivity from interfering with the dowsing process.

How does divining work?

There are many different theories about the mechanism of dowsing. There may be explanations on the physical, emotional, spiritual, electromagnetic, biochemical and many other levels, which explain the same thing in different terms. One explanation is that it is a simple process that connects the rational, intellectual part of ourselves with the intuitive, wise part or Higher Self. It is like a doorway between the mind and the spirit, using the body as a threshold. Dowsing works by sending the unconscious knowledge into the arm muscles, making the L-rods move together or away from each other.

We can use dowsing rods to detect energy patterns in nature, such as the different frequencies or patterns of subtle energy given off by different substances, the Earth energies of different places or electromagnetic fields and Geopathic Stress so we can observe the different effects they have on us. Where ley lines cross are points of power.

How to divine with L-Rods

1. Pick up and hold the L-rods straight out in front of you in a comfortable position. It is important to relax and hold the rods loosely, as gripping them too tightly will prevent the rods from swinging and rotating freely inside the handles. Hold the L-rods at least 6 inches apart, but no wider than shoulder width apart. You may wish to hold your elbows in next to your body for more support. Keep your grip loose and the rods parallel to the floor. Point the rods slightly down at a five-degree angle.
2. Now, relax and take a deep breath. Begin by talking to the rods as if you are talking to your spiritual guides. The first thing you need to do is establish what a "yes" answer looks like by saying, "Show me a yes". Most people get the L-rods to cross, but if the rods want to be wide open for yes, it's okay. Just make sure you always get the same response for a yes answer. Once the L-rods are programmed for a "yes," you are ready to program them for a "no." Repeat the exercise with, "Show me a no." Your intent expressed in the yes/no question will cause the rods to respond with an answer.
3. I always ask for permission to dowse. "May I dowse for the good of the universe and everything within it?", then wait for a 'yes' sign. This takes away any power/ego trips that some may use to the detriment of others. If dowsing for or with others, ask their permission.

Chapter 2: How to use Divining Rods

4. Calm and centre yourself and, standing comfortably with your rods in their neutral position, state what your target is, or what you wish to search for, e.g., earth energies, ley lines, or even a lost item. For example, ask of the rods, 'please show me positive earth energy lines.

5. Walk forwards at a slow but steady pace. When you reach the first target your rods may either split apart or cross over, depending on what you have determined to be the "yes" or "here it is" response. Sometimes both rods might swing to the right or the left, indicating the new direction you should follow. Continue dowsing to find your target.

More information on Dowsing or Divining with Rods can be discovered by contacting the British Society of Dowsers **www.britishdowsers.org**

BELIEVE IN LOVE

Chapter 3
How to use a Divining Pendulum

One of the most commonly used tools for divination or dowsing is a pendulum. The art of using a pendulum is something that anyone can learn and enjoy experimenting with.

What is a pendulum?

A pendulum is a weighted object hung from a single cord, often crystals are used. It's also possible to use other objects such as a favourite necklace, a bead, even a key. The pendulum is a very simple tool and one that lets the user tune in to their intuition. The pendulum acts as a receiver and transmitter of information and moves in different ways in response to questions.

What is divining with a pendulum used for?

Divining with a pendulum can be used in a variety of different ways. In its most simple form, you can use it to answer questions or aid in decision making.

Pendulums can also be used for:
- Healing purposes and identifying allergies such as food intolerances.
- Help in finding lost objects.
- Finding water or ley lines (however, dowsing rods are easier to use for this).

How does pendulum divining work?

A pendulum works by tapping into your intuition and sixth sense. The pendulum acts as a form of receiver and transmitter, from your higher guidance, the infinite intelligence. As the pendulum moves, you gain answers in response to questions – it's best suited to answer 'yes' or 'no' questions. Some people describe the way a pendulum works as being like bringing together the rational and intuitive sides of you (the left and right sides of your brain). When these two elements are brought together, you're able to make decisions using all the sources, rather than just one of them.

Where do the answers come from?

Many people wonder where the answers come from and debate whether it's really working, or just the pendulum responding to the movement of the user's hand. Whilst the pendulum can certainly be made to move with your hand movements, this isn't always the case and after practice you'll get to see why. As with any form of divination, using a pendulum involves a certain degree of faith, belief, and a decidedly open mind, as the answers come from your intuition and from your higher self and the universal intelligence. I usually say the pendulum is a bit like a TV aerial; it picks up small vibrations and magnifies them so you can see the movement. Remember, it's important to relax!

What sort of pendulum do I need?

There are a variety of pendulums available for divining, but you certainly don't have to buy an expensive pendulum to get good results. In fact, the type of pendulum you choose depends in part on what feels right for you. Many people choose to use a crystal pendulum. Clear quartz, for example, is a popular choice, as the crystal is associated with clarity and connecting to a higher purpose. Amethyst, which has a strong connection with the spiritual, is often popular too, as is a pendulum with the calming properties of a rose quartz crystal.

Chapter 3: How to use a Divining Pendulum

Ultimately, whatever your favourite crystal, or the one you feel more drawn to, can be used on a pendulum, if it is rounded or pointed at one end. You can have more than one pendulum if you wish, with different crystals on them, to use on different occasions. When you are starting out for the first time, you can practice the basic concepts by using a do-it-yourself or handmade pendulum if you wish. For example, you could use a rounded glass bead, a metal ball or even a key suspended on the end of a simple piece of cord. When you know you want to try more, you can then upgrade to a professionally made pendulum.

Before you start using a pendulum

Before you embark on having a go at using a pendulum, it's advisable to cleanse it first and charge it with your own energy. The easiest way to cleanse your pendulum for divining is to put it on a windowsill in direct sunlight for a day allowing it to catch the rays of the sun.

To charge it with your energy, hold the pendulum in your hands, closing them around it. Then spend a short time (5 to 15 minutes will be fine) sitting quietly, with your eyes closed, focusing your energy on your pendulum. If you'd like to, you can say a prayer or ask the god of your understanding for their support and guidance when using the pendulum. Once your pendulum is cleansed and charged, it's a good idea to keep it somewhere safe. Many people like to wrap their pendulums in silk or pop them in a small velvet bag for safekeeping.

How to get started with using a pendulum

Anyone can have a go at using a pendulum, but the main criteria are that you need to start with an open mind and put any doubts to one side.

1. The string, chain or cord of the pendulum should be held between your thumb and forefinger in whichever hand feels most comfortable. Some pendulums have a small metal loop or ring at the top of the chain which can make it easy to hold. Ideally the pendulum chain shouldn't be too long, especially when you're first getting started, so if it seems too long or you've got excess string or chord, then you can wrap it lightly around your index finger.
2. When you're ready to start, remember to ask, 'May I dowse for the good of the universe and everything within it?'
3. Sit with your pendulum held between the thumb and forefinger of one hand and run your other hand down the length of the pendulum chain or cord, bringing your hand to rest with the bottom tip of the pendulum in your upturned palm. The pendulum should now be completely still, and you can move your hand away from the bottom of the pendulum. As you move it away, the pendulum will probably start moving. This is perfectly normal. Try and be as relaxed as possible (the more relaxed you are, the better your flow of energy will be) and sit watching the pendulum whilst it moves.
4. After a while it should come to a halt, and you can begin to have a go at determining the 'yes' and 'no' response of your pendulum. Ask your pendulum out loud or in your mind, 'please show me a 'yes' response. Take time to watch the response – it may only be minor at first, but this is normal, as it takes time to get to know how your pendulum interacts with you.
5. Pause for a while, then try the same again asking for the pendulum to show you a 'no' response. Don't worry if you can't tell much difference between the yes and no responses yet – this is perfectly normal at first and you should be able to tell the difference with more practice. For example, some pendulums will make wide circular movements clockwise or anticlockwise in response to 'yes' and one for 'no'. It's helpful to repeat this exercise again, several times, before you're happy with what your 'yes' and 'no' pendulum responses are.
6. Remember, always finish with a 'thank you'.

Chapter 3: How to use a Divining Pendulum

What type of questions can I ask the pendulum?

The pendulum responds better to questions where there are 'yes' or 'no' answers. When you're starting out and practicing, try asking simple questions, like, 'Is today Friday?', 'Is my best friend's name Janet?' or 'Do I live in the UK?' This will help you get a better understanding of how your pendulum responds and help you gain more confidence in using it.

As you get more proficient, you can introduce a 'don't know/can't answer' response for when there is no definite yes or no answer available. You can ask questions about decisions you're making in your personal life, such as whether to buy a certain book, or go to a specific therapist, whether you can trust someone or whether you're eating enough healthy food. You can also try fun exercises, such as locating positive energy/ley lines on a map. Hold the pendulum over different parts of a map and see the responses. As you get more experienced, this method can also be used to locate lost belongings.

More information on Dowsing or Divining with Rods can be discovered by contacting the British Society of Dowsers **www.britishdowsers.org**

Chapter 4
Divining with Your Body

I first learned the art of body divining with my amazing Feng Shui teacher Robert Gray. With body divining you tap into the universal intelligence or divine source of all information, instead of using your logical mind, to acquire your 'yes' or 'no' answers.

You can use this for so much. To assess your authenticity, to assess your current vibration on the Vibe Scale of Consciousness, to assess the vibration of books, magazines, companies, events, therapists, foods, the possibilities for this practice are endless.

To me, body divining is my conscience, my best friend, my oneness with the Universe. I feel I am on the right path when I have used the art of body divining.

So how do you do it?

1.   Stand up, preferably barefoot, toes spread out firmly connecting with the floor. Yogis can stand in mountain pose. Feet shoulder width apart, shoulders back, chest out, chin level and arms by your side. Close your eyes, and ask the Universe, please show me my 'yes'. Stand still and wait. After a few moments your body will rock, usually backwards or forwards.
2.   Say stop.
3.   Start again to find your 'no' answer. Ask the Universe, please show me my 'no'. Again, stand still and wait and after a few moments your body will rock, usually the opposite to your 'yes' answer. If you want to confirm you are on the right track, ask questions you know have 'no' for the answer.

4. When you are happy you have clarity on your 'yes' and 'no' answers, it is always helpful to ask, 'am I connected to my higher self?', or 'do I have permission to ask questions today?' If you get a 'no' answer, then don't do it. Remember only use this skill for the greater good of you, your family, and this earth. Do not use it for any unethical practice.

Chapter 5
How to Discover Your True InnerNature.

Do you know who you are? What is your true inner nature? Why are you here on this planet? What impression are you making on this planet? Do you know your Soul's Purpose?

I have been using the personality profiling tool for over 20 years, it is amazing. It can help you discover your Soul Purpose (your Why), your Emotional Passion (your How) and your Physical Power (your What).

The personality profiling tool is created to help: -

- **People find their authentic power**
- **Singles find their soul mates**
- **Couples consciously connect**
- **Parents understand their children**
- **Families understand each other and have loving open relationships**
- **Employees understand their bosses**
- **Leaders understand their employees, etc.**

The personality profiling tool helps people understand and remove their society conditioning and start them on a journey to find their inner nature, deep inner knowing, fulfilment, satisfaction (happiness). It helps people to understand who they are and why they are here.

This tool looks at Soul Profiles - your unique authentic blueprint, your soul print. Your Soul Profile shows you your Purpose, Passion, and Power which we believe is your profile 100% accurate, as on the day you were born. However, now, due life, to family, peer, and society conditioning etc. it may be much lower. Your Soul Profile provides hope for you to discover your true authentic self.

You are made up of three energies, your trilogy: your Purpose,

Passion, and Power.

1st is your Soul Purpose which clarifies why you do what you do.
2nd is your Emotional Passion which indicates your unique character.
3rd is your Physical Power which is how people see you.

The Golden Circle

A fantastic guy called Simon Sinek (www.simonsinek.com) created a concept he calls the Golden Circle which is basically three circles with a central circle being the 'WHY'. The middle, second circle being the 'HOW' and the third, outer circle being the 'WHAT'. Simon shares how he believes:

Every person knows **WHAT** they do – for example, your job title or function, the products you sell, the services you offer - your physical power

Some people know **HOW** they do it - the actions you take that set you apart from the rest - your inner passion.

Few people know **WHY** they do it - the purpose, the cause or belief that inspires you - your soul purpose.

Soul Purpose (Why)

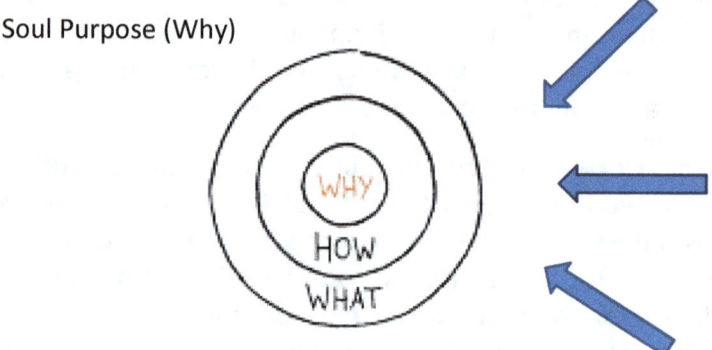

Here are the nine profile types to discover who you, you are

Chapter 5: How to Discover Your True InnerNature.

either: an explorer, a carer, an activist, a pioneer, a connector, a leader, a creator, a teacher, or an illuminator.

Who are you?

Which Tribe are you a member of? Are you:

1. **An EXPLORER - adventurous, sexy, and spiritual**
   Flexible, always fluid, always wants win/win situations, balanced, objective, clarity of vision, gifted speakers, hold people's attention, original idea generators, easy going, laid back and relaxed.

2. **A CARER - the people person, caring, loving nature**
   Careful, thoughtful, affectionate, team player, understanding, practical, focuses on continuously improving their self and others, sympathetic to other's problems, good at developing and keeping useful business contacts, mother to everyone.

3. **An ACTIVIST - the revolutionary**
   Dynamic, active, highly driven, impatient to see quick results, high energy, constantly expresses opinion, direct, thunderous, career orientated, accurate and precise, black and white, excellent memory, solutions orientated.

4. **A PIONEER - sewing seeds of change**
   Warm, positive, enthusiastic, constantly moving like the wind, has big ideas, sees the big picture, thinks globally, tenacious – constantly working towards goals, gentle and can shy from confrontation.

5. **A CONNECTOR - a socialite – BOLD, Powerful**
   Powerful and bold, centre of attention, great changer (yin then yang), wild then calm, forceful, excellent social skills, domineering and controlling.

6. **A LEADER - an ethical Eco warrior – Wellbeing of the world in their hearts**
   Natural Ethical Leaders. Honest, open, and trustworthy, respectful, wise, intuitive, perceptive, superb sense of timing, the controller, the leader, the father figure, speaks with authority, strong moral code with high expectations of others.

7. **A CREATOR - a fun lover, the laughter makers**
   The entertainer, fun, charming, engaging, the host, the comedian, bringer of joy and happiness, needs happy environment, stylish and charismatic, youthful attitude to life, playful.

8. **A TEACHER - a peace maker - STRONG, Courageous**
   Strong solid rock, the mountain of knowledge, the storyteller, dramatist, intelligent, clearheaded, perceptive, doesn't suffer fools.

9. **An ILLUMINATOR - here to illuminate the world**
   Fiery, passionate, impulsive, enthusiastic, bright, expressive, recognition, fame, you can Illuminate the world with your passion.

Understanding people's energy can have a dramatic effect on the way you deal with them and the way you think about them. It can make the difference between a positive relationship and a toxic relationship.

To find yours, or anybody else's Soul Profile, either go to lionel@lionelpalatine.com or try it manually over the following pages.

Find your 1st number - your Soul Purpose – your Why

Chapter 5: How to Discover Your True InnerNature.

Discover which of the nine Soul Profile types you are - find your Soul Purpose here.

Yearly cycles flow from the 4th of February to 3rd of February, so if you are born between the 31st of December and 4th of February treat your birth year as the year before to increase the report's accuracy.

Find the year of your birth and take the figure from the top of the column.

Look that figure up on the following page to determine your real purpose for being and what you will naturally excel in doing.

BELIEVE IN LOVE

9	8	7	6	5	4	3	2	1
1901	1902	1903	1904	1905	1906	1907	1908	1909
1910	1911	1912	1913	1914	1915	1916	1917	1918
1919	1920	1921	1922	1925	1924	1925	1926	1927
1928	1929	1930	1931	1932	1933	1934	1935	1936
1937	1938	1939	1940	1941	1942	1943	1944	1945
1946	1947	1948	1949	1950	1951	1952	1953	1954
1955	1956	1957	1958	1959	1960	1961	1962	1963
1964	1965	1966	1967	1968	1969	1970	1971	1972
1973	1974	1975	1976	1977	1978	1979	1980	1981
1982	1983	1984	1985	1986	1987	1988	1989	1990
1991	1992	1993	1994	1995	1996	1997	1998	1999
2000	2001	2002	2003	2004	2005	2006	2007	2008
2009	2010	2011	2012	2013	2014	2015	2016	2017
2018	2019	2020	2021	2022	2023	2024	2025	2026
2027	2028	2029	2030	2031	2032	2033	2034	2035
2036	2037	2038	2039	2040	2041	2042	2043	2044
2045	2046	2047	2048	2049	2050	2051	2052	2053
2054	2055	2056	2057	2058	2059	2060	2061	2062
2063	2064	2065	2066	2067	2068	2069	2070	2071
2072	2073	2074	2075	2076	2077	2078	2079	2080
2081	2082	2083	2084	2085	2086	2087	2088	2089
2090	2091	2092	2093	2094	2095	2096	2097	2097
2098	2099	2100	2101	2102	2103	2104	2105	2106

Find your 2nd number - your Emotional Passion – your How

Remember your Soul Purpose number from the previous table. You will find your Soul Purpose number on the first row of the table – this identifies which column to take your second number from.

Find your birth date in the first column of the table below to discover your second number, your **Emotional Passion** (your inner child).

Chapter 5: How to Discover Your True InnerNature.

Birth Date	1, 4, 7	2, 5, 8	3, 6, 9
Feb 4th – Mar 5th	8	2	5
Mar 6th – Apr 5th	7	1	4
Apr 6th – May 5th	6	9	3
May 6th – Jun 5th	5	8	2
Jun 6th – Jul 7th	4	7	1
Jul 8th – Aug 7th	3	6	9
Aug 8th – Sep 7th	2	5	8
Sep 8th – Oct 8th	1	4	7
Oct 9th – Nov 7th	9	3	6
Nov 8th – Dec 7th	8	2	5
Dec 8th – Jan 5th	7	1	4
Jan 6th – Feb 3rd	6	9	3

Knowing your own emotional number, and importantly knowing other people's emotional numbers, enables you to create much better communication and connectivity. Essentially you can get an understanding of how people think and feel about the things that affect them. This could be your partner, your children, your parents, your employer, or colleagues. We do far more work with this personality profiling tool in our workshops than we could possibly show here. We have found it to be amazingly accurate, incredibly revealing and a massively powerful tool in understanding relationships.

Find your 3rd number - your Physical Power

Use the chart below to cross reference your birth date and your soul purpose to reveal your full three number combination. You will see that you have already identified the first two numbers.

Your full 3 number combination:
1st – your Soul Purpose
2nd – your Emotional Passion 3rd – your Physical Power

	Feb 4th – Mar 5th	Mar 6th – Apr 5th	Apr 6th – May 5th	May 6th – Jun 5th	Jun 6th – Jul 7th	Jul 8th – Aug 7th	Aug 8th – Sep 7th	Sep 8th – Oct 8th	Oct 9th – Nov 7th	Nov 8th – Dec 7th	Dec 8th – Jan 5th	Jan 6th – Feb 3rd
1 Water	187	178	169	151	142	133	124	115	196	187	178	169
2 Earth	225	216	297	288	279	261	252	243	234	225	216	297
3 Tree	353	344	335	326	317	398	389	371	362	353	344	335
4 Tree	481	472	463	454	445	436	427	418	499	481	472	463
5 Earth	528	519	591	582	573	564	555	546	537	528	519	591
6 Metal	656	647	638	629	611	692	683	674	665	656	647	638
7 Metal	784	775	766	757	748	739	721	712	793	784	775	766
8 Earth	822	813	894	885	876	867	858	849	831	822	813	892
9 Fire	959	941	932	923	914	995	986	977	968	959	941	932

The full three number combination reveals who you were born to be, which is by no means who you may be now. It is a snapshot of how the stars aligned at your time of birth. Life has a way of leading us astray. Family, friends, teachers, colleagues, employers, the media etc. try to make us what they want us to be.

Finding our true self can be a very awakening process and certainly shouldn't be taken lightly.

Have fun discovering yourself, your family, your friends, and your colleagues.

Chapter 6
How to live in a healthy home

The first thing that my Feng Shui teacher Robert Gray taught me was that you first deal with any energy that is life threatening. The most important thing you need to do is remove unwanted energies. His top tips were:

1. Remove geopathic stress
2. Remove any EMF Electromagnetic Radiation and Wi-Fi Microwave Radiation
3. Remove clutter
4. Remove negative energy from yourhome.

In this section we introduce you to the invisible hazards that could be lurking in your home. For a full survey it is important you bring in a professional Healthy Home consultant to deal with these energies and support you, particularly if members of your family become seriously ill.

1. Remove Geopathic Stress

Geo means earth and pathos means suffering or disease.

Some negative earth energies can cause detrimental effects to the immune system and human psyche. Geopathic Stress can rise-up through any buildings including homes, schools, offices, and workplaces, causing the occupants to lose physical strength, energy, emotional stability and happiness. It can also cause serious long-term illnesses.

If we are sleeping, living, or working in such a space, we can feel tired, have headaches or feel uneasy.

People living in travelling communities rarely get cancer as they keep moving all the time.

Research in Germany and France on animals has proved that dogs, horses, and many other animals can suffer, but cats, ants and wasps thrive in Geopathically Stressed space. Some plants, for example ivy, will thrive whereas others suffer - but all humans can suffer.

How serious is it for our health and wellbeing?

Much research has been done that links the presence of Geopathic Stress to many health problems, some as serious as life threatening cancer. Geopathic Stress can also lead to any of the following:

- Sleepless nights
- Learning disabilities in children
- Childhood leukemia
- Chronic serious illnesses such as ME., multiple sclerosis, meningitis, asthma, heart and circulatory problems and rheumatism
- Alzheimer's disease
- Depressive illnesses and other nervous conditions
- S.I.D.S (sudden infant death syndrome or cot death)
- 'Sick Building' Syndrome

Geopathic Stress can also affect you by resulting in feelings of exhaustion, nervousness, loss of appetite, feeling cold, cramps, tingling in arms and legs and chronic fatigue on waking.

Chapter 6: How to live in a healthy home

Sources of Geopathic Stress

1. Earth's magnetic field - fusion and movement of different rocks.
2. Natural disturbance - underground water sources and rivers.
3. Man-made disturbance – mines, fracking, sewers, water pipes, building foundations etc.

A Healthy Home Consultation deals with the energy of space and hence it is vital to detect such energies during the survey. A Healthy Home Consultant will use divining rods to detect any Geopathic Stress and can recommend the correction in your affected space for your health and wellbeing.

2.   Remove EMF Electromagnetic Radiation and Wi Fi Microwave Radiation.

Electromagnetic fields, known as EMFs, are fields of electricity measured in nanoteslas. They invisibly surround us in exterior environments through power lines, electrical sub-stations, radio transmitters, mobile phone masts and railway lines etc.

The European (EU) Parliament and many European governments have been warning citizens about the adverse health effects of electromagnetic and microwave radiation for several years. The Health Protection Agency has used an out-dated safety standard, established 15 years ago. The World Health Organization (WHO) recently declared microwave radiation to be a class 2b carcinogen (this officially means that it might cause cancer). To boost your immune system and to protect the health of yourself and your family (especially children), please take precautions.

Inside our homes, businesses and most buildings, electromagnetic fields surround us as they are emitted from electrical appliances such as computers, printers, microwaves, mobile phones and even wall sockets. This often occurs even when the appliances are not in use.

At a biological level, our bodies communicate chemically and electrically between different cells. Studies have shown that long-term exposure to EMFs compromises the immune system by interfering with healthy cell-to-cell communication. They also affect the body's ability to produce essential enzymes and hormones to prevent serious illnesses and over time this can prove detrimental to our health and wellbeing.

Certain health problems have been consistently associated with EMFs in numerous studies performed internationally. Some findings show the incidence of leukaemia to be four times greater where a child's bed is situated in a space with an EMF of 20 volts per metre. Similarly, for adults, incidents of M.E. were found to be three times greater where EMFs of 20 volts per metre or above were measured in sleeping areas.

Safe levels and useful tips for reducing the exposure to EMF:

Normal/acceptable level	Type of Field	High/unacceptable level
Under 5 Volts per metre	Electrical	10+ (not good) 20 + (really bad)
Under 0.05 nanotesla	Magnetic	0.2

Recommendations:
- Ensure all family members are sitting as far away from large electrical items as possible.
- Ensure your PC is fitted with a low radiation monitor and sit at least 1 metre away from the monitor with your legs

Chapter 6: How to live in a healthy home

well away from the cables.
- Minimize use of mobile phones or DECT phones (the ones with wireless handsets that charge on a base unit).
- Sit at least 2 to 3 metres away from TV screens depending on the screen size and place an amethyst crystal on it to absorb the radiation.
- Route broadband through your electrical circuit by installing dLAN Devolo adapters to use all around your house with laptops and PCs. **Do not use Wi-Fi.**

For a better connection...

...lose the wifi

To boost your immune system and to protect the health of yourself and your family (especially children), please take precautions: -
REPLACE: REDUCE: REPOSITION

1. **REPLACE**

- **Replace DECT cordless phones** with wired phones (landlines). DECT cordless phone base emits microwave all day long, whether there are calls or not.
- **Replace Wi-Fi network** with wired computer network: just get a cable for connection. Even laptop computers can be connected to the internet with cables. Radio-frequency signals are always the strongest if broadcasted from inside your own home, so removing your Wi-Fi router helps even if you cannot avoid your neighbours' Wi-Fi coverage. You can also print out this information and pass to your neighbours, to share the information with them.
- **Replace microwave oven** with conventional cooker, toaster, or stove top for cooking - the food tastes better, too!

2. **REDUCE**

- **Limit mobile phone use** to essential calls and keep calls short. Send text messages instead of making calls whenever possible. Use wired landline for long chats that are not urgent.
- **Set mobile phone to "aeroplane"** mode when you don't need it, to suspend connection and radiation temporarily.
- If it's not possible to hardwire computers because of physical limitations at the location, and dLan is not possible either, then **turn on Wi-Fi only when you need to use i**t and turn it off especially overnight. Some have found it helpful to use an adapter with timer to turn

Chapter 6: How to live in a healthy home

on/off Wi-Fi router automatically at pre-set hours. Note that while Wi-Fi is on, each router continuously broadcasts 2.4 billion cycles of microwave per second into its surroundings. This frequency penetrates walls and human bodies.

- **Say NO to "Smart Meters"** which emit microwaves at every house in the entire area.

3. **REPOSITION**

- Wireless devices (mobile phones, smart phones, iTouch, iPads, Wi-Fi-enabled laptops etc.) emit the highest amount of radiation during talk-time or data transmission. Therefore, keep devices on the table or holder rather than on your lap or in your hands, and away from the head, while in communication. Talk with air-tube, speakerphone or wired headset.
- If you use bluetooth while talking and keep the phone in your pocket at the same time, you'll get maximum absorption of the radiation at your head and your body.
- Carry mobile phones in handbags or brief cases instead of in pockets against your body: Microwave radiation causes infertility and, for pregnant women, affects the brain development of the foetus.
- **Keep mobile phones and Wi-Fi-enabled devices away from children and babies.**
- Do not position a Wi-Fi router or cordless phone base close to your brain, e.g., at bedside table or at your desk near head level.
- **When you sleep, don't place a mobile phone or radio alarm clock at bedside. Turn off your mobile phone.**
- **Avoid using digital baby monitors.** If it's absolutely required, then avoid placing the units near the bedside or against the body of you or your baby. Position it at the other side of the room.

Please, please, please act and boost your immune system and to protect the health of yourself and your family (especially children), please take precautions.

I would like to thank our Toxin Free Communities team for inspiring me to share this information in our book. Lionel and I live in a Toxin Free House, we do not have Wi Fi - our internet is streamed through our electricity cables. We do not have SMART meters etc. I sincerely hope you act and Replace, Reduce and Reposition.

Radiation really does play havoc with your immune system so keep strong and take action to protect your health and the health of your family (especially children).

3. Clear Your Clutter

Free yourself of clutter and remove negativity from your home.

Clutter can be an actual physical collection of things you do not use or love, things that are untidy and disorganized, too many things in a small place or an unfinished task or unused items. Clutter can also exist in our conscious and subconscious mind. It represents the energy, which is stuck in our inner and outer worlds that prevents us from moving on in life. Clutter is the biggest enemy or obstruction to creating good Feng Shui in any environment.

You may find physical clutter everywhere in any room of your home. In cupboards, the loft, the garage and usually the shed. We find it in hallways, passages, under beds, on top of wardrobes, in handbag pockets, in the car, the office, the fridge and even in the food cupboards.

Clutter around you makes you feel tired. Clear your clutter to feel lighter in body, mind, and spirit. Your home is a mirrored reflection of your lifestyle and each area of your home is connected to a different aspect of your life. The area in which the clutter gets collected can adversely affect that area of your life.

Tips for clearing the clutter:

- **Start small**. If you have a lot of clutter, tackle one shelf of your cupboard at a time and give yourself a treat when you have done it!
- Ensure that others in your home take responsibility to clear their own clutter rather than you doing it for them.
- **Change old habits** – stop keeping things 'in case they come in useful'.
- Ensure that you have a 'home' for every single item in your house – if this is the case then it is impossible to have clutter.
- If something is broken, fix it-or throw it out. Your energy levels drop when you are surrounded by things that do not work properly.
- **Clear your wardrobe**. We normally wear 20% of our clothes 80% of the time. Give away the ones you do not need and buy only the clothes you absolutely love. When you look good, you feel good, and your life works better.
- **Clear the clutter from corridors and behind the doors**. Your life will proceed more smoothly when the energy flows unobstructed around your space.
- **Clear your desk in the study**. Mountains of paperwork can defeat you even before you start. A clear desk means clarity of thought, more creativity and better satisfaction.
- Bring yourself up to date. Watch your energy levels soar when you write your pending letters and make the outstanding calls.

- Finally, clear your clutter before implementing Feng Shui cures and enhancements such as crystals, mirrors, plants, or anything, otherwise you may double your problems rather than solve them!

Remember - everything grows except the size of our home. So, when you buy something new, discard something old to avoid clutter.

Remove all items that represent loneliness or singularity, all pictures of individuals or paintings that may project sorrow or isolation, whether directly or inferred through specific times or the events of buying them.

Remove the items that may cause anxiety and further suffering as you cling on to images of previous memory patterns - so be prepared, it can stir up many emotions.

Replace emptiness with images of love, union, togetherness, and connectedness. This alone will instill your subconscious mind with joy. We need a positive attitude in everything we do, so we don't miss the opportunity of meeting the right person who will be our equal.

4. **Clear Your Home of Negative Energy.**

It is energy 'left' by visitors or previous owners of your home that you may not want to be permanent within your living space. It is particularly beneficial to remove negative predecessor energy in the following instances:

- After moving into a new or different house
- After a serious illness in the home and/or to promote healing
- After a relationship break-up, divorce, or serious argument

Chapter 6: How to live in a healthy home

- When you have had a lot of visitors (especially unwanted ones!)
- If you feel 'stuck' in yourlife
- When you want to make a new start

An analogy that is a useful way to think about when you move into a new or different house without removing the negative predecessor energy is **'like putting a new bunch of flowers into dirty vase water'** i.e., you are moving into someone else's old energy vibrations.

Please go to Chapter 8 of this section (Step 2) for more information.

How to clear your home of negative energy

My year-long Feng Shui Practitioner training inspired me and immersed me in each area we'd had a taste of during the foundation weekend. I completed the full training course in Buxton, the most gorgeous spa town, where I loved to drink from the fresh springs every day, this natural water was so incredibly refreshing.

I finished the course in the year 2000. At this time, I was still running my Environmental Transformation Company. I used what I had learned within my home and within my business. Oh, wow was I excited to do this, it worked so well, the positive results I achieved were a testimony to the power of Feng Shui.

In 2003 I went to Bali to study the principles of Clutter Clearing and Space Clearing. Oh, la la, that was so enlightening. Some of the things I experienced were 'out of this world.' I studied with a lady called Karen Kingston. Here are a few of the things that surprised me:

1. Karen said, "All of the attendees on this Clutter Clearing course will find that your close family back home will be clutter clearing while you are here", it was like we had a telepathic connection with the family back home.
2. On the Space Clearing 'Energy Sensing' course Karen taught us how to sense colours with our hands. Many of us found the ability to tune in completely and identified the correct colours 10 out of 10 times.
3. Karen trained us how to sensitize our hands to feel energies in rooms, to feel stuck energies in corners and to feel electricity cables in walls and plugs etc. This was such an awakening.
4. Karen introduced us to our aura, and we assessed the size of one another's auras too. It was fascinating. She enlightened us to the effect a mobile phone has on our auras. How they can negatively affect us was a real shock to me.

Karen organized a purification ceremony for us with a Balinese priest. We all gathered in a room for the ceremony to take place. One by one we went up to meet him and one by one he scanned our bodies with his third eye. He could tell us what ailments and issues we had in our body. I was astounded at his accuracy. He found where everyone had previously broken bones, where their aches and pains were. One lady with Fibromyalgia was cured in a few moments after some deep acupressure massage on her neck. This lady had been exhausted throughout our course but the following days after the ceremony she was full of vitality.

One joyous day Karen took us to a Balinese temple, high up in the mountains called Batukaru to experience a Blessing Ceremony where we would be blessed by the priests. She explained the Balinese Ritual of Blessings. I felt very different after I had been blessed. I felt pure, enlightened and at peace.

Chapter 6: How to live in a healthy home

It was as if I could feel the sacred energy of the temple, it was so beautiful.

I have shared my learnings with Lionel, and every year on the 5th February we perform the ritual outlined next.

Remove negative energy and refresh your home by atmospheric cleansing

What is it? Atmospheric cleansing is a method of cleansing any space of old, harmful, or stagnant energy and then re- infusing the space with new, fresh energies to revitalize living spaces. It also removes any energy 'left' by visitors or previous owners of your home that you may not want to be permanent within your living space. It is not connected with any specific religion or belief. Space clearing as it's also known, has been undertaken in homes, offices, schools, hospitals and even cars!

Why cleanse your home? It revitalizes and raises the energy in the space and in doing so raises the quality of your life. Feedback from those who have had their homes spaced cleared frequently say that they have a sense of oneness with their home and feel peaceful, radiant, happy, and safe after it has been cleared.

It is particularly beneficial to space clear in the following instances:
- After moving into a new or different house
- After a serious illness in the home and/or to promote healing
- After a relationship break-up, divorce, or serious argument
- When you have had a lot of visitors (especially unwanted ones!)
- If you feel 'stuck' in your life

BELIEVE IN LOVE

- When you want to make a new start
- To ensure any residual harmful earth energy (Geopathic Stress) is cleared

Space clearing has three main stages:
- Purification – removing the old energies.
- Invocation – filling your home with your energy, your wishes, and dreams.
- Preservation – sealing in the positive energy.

People who work with acoustics are aware of how energy gets 'trapped' in corners. It is the same principal with energy in homes, it can be effectively 'stored' for years in walls and particularly corners.

Space clearing involves activity and use of intention. A combination of the physical (for example the writing of a wish list) and the metaphysical (for example a visualization of positive nurturing energy filling the home).

A quick lesson in atmospheric clearing

What you need:
1. A table to make your offerings for each room (make it pretty with beautiful cloths etc.)
2. Sage or incense
3. Bells, drums, or rattles
4. Balinese harmony balls, Kochi bells, gentle fine bells, shakers or rose quartz crystals
5. Sacred spring water or inject your own water with love
6. Saucers or side plates to make offerings. One for each room of your house.
7. Tea lights for each plate
8. Matches or lighter
9. Flowers in season, or buy your favourite flowers to make offerings

Chapter 6: How to live in a healthy home

Purification by Sound
Lionel and I always do three circuits of the internal perimeter of our home clearing, cleansing, and harmonizing the energy.

Circuit 1 – Clearing the Atmosphere with dried sage or incense
Circuit 2 – Cleansing the Atmosphere by clapping into every nook, cranny, and corner
Circuit 3 – Harmonizing the Atmosphere with bells

Invocation by Earth, Water, Air and Fire

We use the elements and perform ceremonies in each room of the house. Create your own offering to the spirits of the house and its space. We use side plates and put a tea light on them. We gather flowers and contributions from nature to make the offerings, this can be anything from flowers, pinecones to berries, whatever is in season, grabs your attention or is meaningful to you.

Assemble a table in what you feel is the power position of the house, where the whole house can feel its presence. Make your table beautiful. Adorn it with special items sacred to you. Maybe deities, crystals, pictures of your family or your lover.

Lay out all the offerings / plates you need. One for each room and a mistress or master offering / plate to stay on the main table. Put a tea light on each plate. Create offerings by placing flowers on the plates and whatever you feel is relevant (take care not to put anything adjacent to the candle just in case it catches fire).

Light the mistress or master candle to commence your ceremony to bless the house with your love. When you light the candle, dream, and visualize all the beauty, love, light, peace and happiness you want to feel in your house.

Now take your matches, and with each offering do the same in each room of your house. Ensure you put the plate down in a safe position preferably central to the room. Light the candle, dream and visualize all the beautiful things you want to happen in that room.

Repeat for every room.

Preservation by Intention, Light and Love

Your role is to put into the ether all your intentions, wishes and dreams of what you want to happen in your home and life and to fill your home with light and love.

We like to do a meditation to implant our dreams into Harmony Balls' whilst holding them in our hands. Then we do two more final circuits.

Circuit 4 - Injecting your wishes and dreams
We dance around the perimeters of our home ringing the Harmony Balls to implant our intentions firmly into each room and the whole house.

Circuit 5 - Purification of space
On the final circuit we sprinkle sacred spring water to purify our space.

Our last action is to gently scatter flower petals at each of the entrances, sprinkle sacred spring water over them and perform a special blessing for our future love and happiness.

We recommend you read Karen Kingston's wonderful book 'Creating Sacred Space'.

Chapter 6: How to live in a healthy home

You can buy harmony balls by emailing
lionel@lionelpalatine.com

Chapter 7
How to Live in a Happy Home

Happy Home Zones

There are nine Home Energy Zones used in our Happy Home Consultations. These are:

1. **Purpose** – Your life's journey, your career
2. **Love** and relationships
3. **Health,** family and respecting your elders
4. **Abundance**, prosperity, wealth
5. **Harmony** - Your wellbeing
6. **People**, friends, mentors
7. **Happiness**, children, creativity
8. **Peace**, wisdom, quiet contemplation
9. **Passion**, success, fame, illumination

The eight outer zones correspond to one of the eight points on a compass. Zone five is the harmonious middle. Each zone identifies a section of your home relating to a different aspect of your life. Symbolic and elemental cures can enhance these areas of your life and family.

I would like to introduce you to five elements we work with in Feng Shui: - Water, Wood, Fire, Earth, and Metal. Each of the nine zone in your home are represented by one of these elements. You can enhance and create auspicious energy in each of these areas, by using characteristics that nurture the essential elements of each area or Home Energy zone.

I have created a chart for you so you can evaluate which of your life areas need addressing:

Life Area	☹️ Very Poor Needs Attention	🙂 Excellent Needs No Attention
1. Purpose Life's Journey	I feel like I'm swimming against the tide. I don't like my job. I'm thinking of changing career. I am out of work and finding it difficult to get a job.	I feel that my life is flowing along well. I'm on the right path. I really like my work. I feel fortunate to be doing what I really want to do.
2. Love Relationships	I feel isolated and lonely. I do not have a partner and there are no 'would-be' partners asking me out. I'm unhappy in my relationship and thinking of separation/divorce. I've had a string of bad relationships.	I have a fulfilling relationship with my partner. My partner gives me lots of love and attention. I have a good social life with lots of 'would-be' partners asking me out. I feel loved all the time. I find it easy to love.
3. Health Family Elders	I have / had a difficult relationship with one or both of my parents. I don't see / speak to my parents very often. I'm unhappy in relation to my past. I don't get on well with my boss.	I have / had a good relationship with both of my parents. I see / speak to my parents often. I'm happy in relation to my past. I respect my elders. I get on well with my boss.

Chapter 7: How to Live in a Happy Home

4. Abundance Wealth	I feel I'm having bad luck at the moment. Money is tight / non-existent. My income is insufficient to meet my outgoings. I have debts that need clearing.	Good fortune occurs readily in my life. I make a good income and cash flow is not a problem. I feel lucky and others view me as lucky. Things tend to show up just when I need them.
5. Harmony Well-Being	My physical, mental, or emotional health is poor. I have no energy. My memory and / or concentration are poor. I feel emotionally unstable / insecure.	My physical, mental, emotional health is good. I have lots of energy. My memory and concentration are good. I feel emotionally secure.
6. People Friends Mentors	I always seem to be alone. I have few friends. I neither have the time or money to give to others who are in need. Friends don't call on me for help / support.	In times of need my friends are always there for me. People seem to turn up just when I need them. I am generous and supportive with both my time and money. Friends turn to me for help.
7. Happiness Children Creativity	I have no children and don't like them. I want children but haven't been able to conceive. I have children, but we don't get on very well. I don't feel creative.	I don't have children, but love those of others. I have lovely children, and they are my life. I am very creative with my work and / or hobbies.

8. Peace Wisdom Quiet Contemplation	I have little or no time for quiet contemplation. My head is always busy, and I find it difficult to clear my thoughts. I feel stressed most of the time. My life is practical and monotonous.	I find time daily to be by myself. I meditate (or walk, do yoga or Tai Chi, etc.) on a regular basis, and find it easy to clear my thoughts. I feel calm most of the time. My life is a beautiful spiritual journey.
9. Passion, Success, Fame Illumination	I'm unclear as to my purpose in life. I gain little pleasure from life. I do not feel fulfilled. I never seem to be recognized / appreciated for the work that I do.	I am clear as to my purpose in life. I enjoy my life. I feel fulfilled in what I do. I am highly respected in my work. I feel respected / valued as a human being.

Just use your honest judgement to indicate on the following chart where you feel you are right now on a scale of 1 to 10 for each area. The scores that you choose are a guide for you to identify the priority of attention.

Please circle one number between 1 and 10 for each life area:

Life Area	Priority Level									
1. Purpose	1	2	3	4	5	6	7	8	9	10
2. Love	1	2	3	4	5	6	7	8	9	10
3. Health	1	2	3	4	5	6	7	8	9	10
4. Abundance	1	2	3	4	5	6	7	8	9	10
5. Harmony	1	2	3	4	5	6	7	8	9	10

Chapter 7: How to Live in a Happy Home

6. Friends	1	2	3	4	5	6	7	8	9	10
7. Happiness	1	2	3	4	5	6	7	8	9	10
8. Peace Wisdom	1	2	3	4	5	6	7	8	9	10
9. Recognition	1	2	3	4	5	6	7	8	9	10

Having completed the previous chart which of the following three areas would you like to prioritize? I suggest you pick your top three Life Areas that need to be worked on.

Priority 1 Life Area:
Priority 2 Life Area:
Priority 3 Life Area:

You then need to create a simple plan of your home and place the home zone chart, from the next page, over your plan to show the relevant areas.

1. Create a floor plan for downstairs and one for upstairs (if appropriate).
2. Find the compass direction North and mark it on the plan.
3. Place the zone chart over the plan so that Zone 1 North corresponds to the compass direction North.
4. Divide your home into nine equal zones and write in the Life Areas for each zone.

Home Zone Chart

4 SOUTH EAST **ABUNDANCE** Gratitude Wealth Late Spring Mid-Morning **Wood** Green Wind Female Eldest Daughter	9 SOUTH **PASSION** Fame & Reputation Mid-Summer Mid-Day **Fire** Red Fire Female Middle Daughter	2 SOUTH WEST **LOVE** Relationships & Marriage Late Summer Early Afternoon **Earth** Yellow, terracotta Earth Female Matriarch, Mother
3 EAST **HEALTH** Family & New Beginnings Spring Sunrise **Wood** Green Thunder Male Eldest Son	5 CENTRE **HARMONY** Wellbeing and Health Tai Chi Centre **Earth** Yellow	7 WEST **HAPPINESS** Creativity, Children, Joy Future Early Autumn Mid Afternoon **Metal** Gold, Silver, White Lake Female Youngest Daughter
8 NORTH EAST **PEACE** Wisdom and Knowledge Late Winter Very Early Morning **Earth** Yellow, terracotta Mountain Male Youngest Son	1 NORTH **PURPOSE** Life'sJourney Mid-Winter Mid Night **Water** Blue Black Water Male Middle Son	6 NORTH WEST **PEOPLE** Helpful Friends, Mentors, Travel Late Autumn Evening **Metal** Gold, Silver, White Heaven Male Patriarch, Father

Chapter 7: How to Live in a Happy Home

Each zone carries an energy that can be either instrumental or detrimental to everything you want in life. By working with your environment whether at home or work, in a manner that allows the energy to flow in the right direction, you are better able to overcome challenges and secure the route to success of your ultimate purpose.

Water (1) nurtures Wood (3,4)
Wood (3,4) nurtures Fire (9)
Fire (9) nurtures Earth (2,5.8)
Earth (2,5,8) nurtures Metal (6,7)
Metal (6,7) nurtures Water (1)
And the cycle continues...

Here is a guide to how you can enhance each of the nine zones.

1: Purpose
Life's Journey
The energy in this zone is that of study, planning, research, conserving and quiet.

        Direction = North
        Element = Water
        Symbolism = Water
        Family Member = Middle Son
        Season = Winter
        Enhancer = Colours: blue or black; flowing river, boats, water fountain, pictures of running water flowing towards you. Water must be fresh and healthy.

2: Love
Relationships
The energy in this zone is that of stillness, germination, preparation, planting, clearing the past excess and changing.

        Direction = South West
        Element = Earth
        Symbolism = Earth
        Family Member = Mother
        Season = Late Summer / Early Autumn
        Enhancer = Colours: earth, terracotta, orange, red. Enhance with element of fire, candles (2), pictures of couples (especially dressed in red), statues of the lovers. Gustav Klimt 'Kiss' picture on the wall.

3: Health
Family and elders (place of ancestral connection)
The energy in this zone is that of sprouting, initiation, luck, growth and new projects.

Direction = East
Element = Strong Wood
Symbolism = Thunder
Family Member = Eldest Son
Season = Spring
Enhancers = Colours: all shades of green, or blue. Enhance area with healthy rounded leaved plants that are kept watered well. Pictures of your family and elders on walls.

4: Abundance
Wealth / Fortunate Blessing
The energy of this zone is that of rapid growth, blossoming and movement without stability.

Direction = South East
Element = Gentle Wood
Symbolism = Wind
Family Member = Eldest Daughter
Season = Late Spring
Enhancers = Colour: green. Enhancers are succulent money plants (4) keep them healthy. Rounded leaved plants, plants that inspire you and are uplifting like palms or peace lilies.
Do not use artificial plants!

5: Harmony
Wellbeing / Unity
The energy of this zone is harmonious, this is the tai chi of your home, please keep it clutter free.

Direction = Centre
Element = Earth

Symbolism =Tai Chi
Family Member =None
Season =None
Enhancers =Colour neutral, creams, earthy faun colours. Keep this area really free from clutter, minimalistic, not much in this area at all, ensure energy can flow.

6: People

Partnership / Courage — Helpful Friends / Mentors

The energy in this zone is that of harvest, prosperity, gathering, authority and beneficial connection.

Direction =North West
Element =Strong Metal
Symbolism =Heaven
Family Member =Father
Season =Late Autumn
Enhancers =Colours: gold, silver, white.
Pictures of friends - ensure they are positive and uplifting. Pictures of your gurus i.e. Dalai Lama, Gandhi. Metal objects particularly curvaceous rounded metal artworks and sculptures. I love the shiny metal spheres in this zone.
Also, your favourite crystals and rocks can go in this zone too.

7: Happiness

Creativity / Children

The energy of this zone is of celebration, joy, and gratitude, relaxed and not serious.

Direction =West
Element =Gentle Metal
Symbolism =Lake
Family Member =Youngest Daughter

Season = Autumn
Enhancers = Colours gold, silver, white. Pictures of happy children. This is the creative zone so you can install your favourite art in this area or your own art. Also, your favourite crystals and rocks can go in this zone too. This is the zone to put pictures of your children, or grandchildren etc. Children bring pure innocent happiness into your life.

8: Peace
Wisdom / Knowledge
The energy of this zone is that of stillness, calm before the storm, uncommunicative like going into a cave and self-reflection.

Direction = South West
Element = Earth
Symbolism = Mountain
Family Member = Youngest Son
Season = Late Winter
Enhancers = Colours: earthy terracotta, orange, earth colours. This is an earth element so beautiful statues that emit the feeling of peace i.e. Buddha statues or other spiritual symbolism.

9: Passion
Fame / Illumination / Recognition
The energy of this zone is that of recognition, fame, very busy, everything coming to the surface as if you are placed under a magnifying glass.

Direction = South
Element = Fire

Symbolism =Fire
Family Member =Middle Daughter
Season =Summer
Enhancers =Colours: red, pink, purple, magenta. Also, can be enhanced with green. This zone needs a picture of you dressed in red doing what you want to be famous for. This is the zone to light candles, a great place to have an altar and to light candles every day to give gratitude and also, set clear intentions of what you want to happen. Fire Zone makes it happen.

By working with the energy of the environment you will also be more attuned to your purpose and will produce and create more.

We are influenced by everything we connect to around us

Your environment should be an uplifting, happy place, not sad or depressing. We can change the inner landscape of people by changing their outer environment. Symbolism is therefore very important in your home and place of work too.

We are surrounded by symbols. Everything in our homes and workplaces says something about us to everyone who sees it, be it your family, friends, clients, colleagues, or your staff. The objects surrounding us in our homes and offices continually give messages to us at our subconscious level. This affects our thought processes and ultimately our behaviour. It is therefore important to use symbolism in a positive and life- enhancing way.

Every single object in your home and workplace, whether it is artwork, sculpture, piece of furniture, furnishing or decorative ornament can be categorized into a symbolic element to tell

Chapter 7: How to Live in a Happy Home

whether it is positively supportive to the occupants of the premises. Check and see what negative and positive messages are given by the artwork in your home and workplace. Are they dull, flat and limiting landscapes? Sunsets, showing declining energy? Stark aggressive images? Abstract lines without clarity? Improve the energy to improve your life.

- Negative images include battle scenes, sinking ships, daggers, missiles, sunsets or anything dead e.g. plant, fish, animal or people.
- Positive images include birds flying, sunrise, flowers, gardens, and landscapes.

We live in a vibrational world. Just like a lamp lights up when the connection is made to the wall socket through the flick of a switch, our destiny is influenced by everything we connect to around us.

Symbolism in our homes

In 2005, I travelled to Malaysia to study Feng Shui with Lillian Too, the woman who brought Feng Shui to the Western World. Here I passed the exams to become a Master Feng Shui Practitioner.

The key learning, I took from this course was the importance of symbolism, of what you surround yourself with in your home and work. Lillian owned Feng Shui shops that were full of trinkets and symbols for every possible thing you can think of. Only two items really resonated with me.

Kuan Kung sculptures (below). He is a warrior who offers protection to those who let him in, he protects from negative energies. I bought one for my business and one for my home. I have positioned them facing the main doorways to keep the places safe and protected.

The second symbol which I adore is the infinity knot. I purchased 200 jade infinity knots on red rope to share with friends and family. Lillian told us that if ever we needed a taxi, to just rub our infinity knot and a taxi will come. I've tried and tested this so many times and it's worked every time. Wow! Don't ask me how.

Chapter 7: How to Live in a Happy Home

My favourite symbolic painting is by Gustav Klimt which originally was called 'The Lovers' and latterly named 'The KISS'. I used this picture throughout my workplace as I personally believed and connected this painting with KISS Keep It Simple and Sexy. I also used this painting and hung it in my bedroom above my bed head when I was ready to manifest my soul mate - it worked.

BELIEVE IN LOVE

Chapter 8
How to Create the Life of Your Dreams - Dream Board Creation

Creating an inspirational dream board is probably one of the most valuable visualization tools available to you. This powerful tool serves as your image of the future - a tangible representation of where you are going. It represents your dreams, your goals, and your ideal life and loves. Creating a Dream Board will help you create the life of your dreams, make your dreams a reality.

Because your mind responds strongly to visual stimulation - by representing your goals with words, pictures, and images - you will strengthen and stimulate your emotions. Your emotions are the vibrational energy that activates the manifestation process - if you have already defined your dreams, it's time to illustrate them visually.

How to do it

Find either a cork board, or a large piece of cardboard to create your dream board on. Obtain a pencil and ruler and mark out the nine sections to manifest your dreams. You could also do this digitally i.e. on PowerPoint or Pinterest for those digitally competent.

Here is our suggested layout as per Life Energy Zones

ABUNDANCE PROSPERITY WEALTH	**PASSION** RECOGNITION FAME	**LOVE** PARTNER RELATIONSHIP
HEALTH FAMILY NATURE	**HARMONY** BALANCE WELLBEING	**HAPPINESS** CREATIVITY CHILDREN
PEACE WISDOM SPIRITUALITY	**PURPOSE** CAREER SOUL DESTINY	**PEOPLE** COURAGE FRIENDS

Find pictures that represent or symbolize the experiences, feelings, and people you want to attract into your life and place them in your board. Have fun with the process! Use photographs, magazine cut outs, pictures from the Internet-- whatever inspires you. Be creative. Include not only pictures, but anything that speaks to you.

Include a picture of yourself in your board. If you can, choose one that was taken in a happy moment. You will also want to post your affirmations, inspirational words, quotations, and thoughts here. Choose words and images that inspire you and make you feel good.

Use your dream board to depict goals and dreams in all nine areas of your life. Keep it neat and be selective about what you place on your dream board. It's a good idea to avoid creating a cluttered or chaotic board... you don't want to attract chaos into your life.

Chapter 8: How to Create the Life of Your Dreams - Dream Board Creation

Use only the words and images that best represent your purpose, your ideal future, and words that inspire positive emotions in you. There is beauty in simplicity and clarity. Too many images and too much information will be distracting and harder to focus on.

When you are working on visualizing and creating changes in many areas of your life, you may want to use more than one dream board. You might use one for your personal dreams and another for your business dreams and aspirations. You might even want to keep your business dream board at the office or on your desk as a means of inspiration and affirmation.

How to use your dream board

We recommend you put your dream board where you see it first thing in the morning and last thing at night.

Spend time each morning and evening visualizing, affirming, believing, and internalizing your dreams.

The time you spend visualizing in the evening just before bed is especially powerful. The thoughts and images that are present in your mind during the last minutes before going to sleep, are the ones that will replay themselves repeatedly in your subconscious mind throughout the night, and the thoughts and images that you begin each day with will help you to create a vibrational match for the future you desire.

As some time goes by, and your dreams begin to manifest, look at those images that represent your achievements, and feel gratitude for how well your manifestation process is working in your life. Acknowledge that it is working. Don't remove the pictures or images that represent the dreams you've already achieved. Achievement of the goals in your inspirational dream board are powerful visual reminders of what you have already consciously and deliberately attracted into your life.

We recommend you write down the date you created your vision board. The universe loves speed, and you will be amazed at just how quickly the manifestation process responds to your energy, commitment, and desires. Much like a time capsule, this board will document your personal journey, your dreams, and your achievements for that particular year. It will become a record of your growth, awareness, and expansion that you will want to keep and reflect upon in years to come.

It's a good idea to create a new vision board each year. As you continue to grow, evolve, and expand, your dreams will too. Your empowering dream board is meant to be kept and cherished. They chronicle not only your dreams, but your growth and achievements.

Using your Dream Board

- Look at your dream board often and feel the inspiration it provides.
- Hold it in your hands and really internalize the future it represents.
- Read your affirmations and inspirational words aloud.
- See yourself living in that manner.
- Feel yourself in the future you have created.
- Believe it is already yours.
- Be grateful for the good that is already present in your life.
- Acknowledge the changes you have seen and felt.
- Look at it just before going to bed and first thing upon rising.

We hope we've inspired you to create your own inspirational dream board. Your ability to visualize your dreams will serve as a catalyst in their creation.

Chapter 8: How to Create the Life of Your Dreams - Dream Board Creation

It's also most important is to be grateful for your life and all you are manifesting.

Jot some ideas of pictures and words you want to put in each Life Area of your Dream Board here: -

Abundance	Passion	Love
Health	Harmony	Happiness
Peace	Purpose	People

Chapter 9
How to be a Pearl Fisher

While the spiritual journey I write about in this book started in 2000, I had my first taste of it back in 1989. My partner at that time worked for Shell International and every recruit at Shell had to attend a Time Manager International Course. My partner went on the course and returned so enthused, he exclaimed, "Dawn, you need to go on this course".

The aim of the course was to help you get the most out of your life. It showed you how to set life goals and plan how you were going to achieve them. It also taught many life skills to bring health and happiness into your life. The two skills I remember were:

1. **How to Eat Elephants** (Big Projects). You cut them up into small bite-size chunks so you can digest and make them happen.
2. **Pearl Fishing.** It just amazed me, so much so, I closed my company for two days and gifted every member of my team to this two-day experience.

What is Pearl Fishing

Pearl Fishing is a state of mind, it is your attitude. The key to Pearl Fishing is when you meet someone, always look for the beauty in that person and if possible, appropriately compliment that person so it makes them feel good. Wow, what a difference that makes to your life.

It also makes you smile from your heart as you keep doing it. Life gets more pleasant. Us Brits have a reputation of having a stiff upper lip and always moaning about the weather. With

Pearl Fishing, even if it is raining, you will bring rays of sunshine into people's lives.

As part of the course, we also learned about the Pearl Crushers. There are too many Pearl Crushers. These are the people who always look on the dark side of life, and moan about all aspects of their life, even aspects which are out of their control. So please join me and become a Pearl Fisher, it will transform your life, I promise.

I want to share with you one more jewel from that course. When you arrive home from work, stop outside your front door, and leave your work outside. Stand and think, 'what beautiful things do I want to happen tonight with my family?'

This is how Edward Scheldrick, our teacher, greets his wife. "Hi Honey, Tiger's home". That brought a smile to all our faces.

The spark I felt on this course was my first taste of how good it feels to really be conscious and present with everyone I meet. It made a real difference. My job then as Managing Director was transformed, I created a new way of leadership, leading all my team using these techniques. It worked and we went from strength to strength.

This course changed the culture of my company, everyone practiced this positive way of communicating, catching people doing things right and seeing their beauty and strengths.

Chapter 10
How to Calm Your Mind with Mantras

The Magic of Mantras

In 2012, Lionel and I went on a course run by the Bright Path Ishayas called the Ishaya Ascension 3-day course. It impacted us tremendously, particularly in finding inner peace. I highly recommend the introductory course as it is so simple.

You are taught how to develop a unique mind mantra, your own words which you say repeatedly in your mind. On the course, we enjoyed this for hours and hours. It removes all the mind's chatter, distractions, worries and thoughts.

You can create your own mantra of course. Be creative, I've used mantras in my public speaking to large manufacturing audiences, I would ask thousands of people to stand up and chant these words:

> We are strong We are powerful
> We are magnificent

I asked them to chant this mantra five times and really feel it. Wow, it was a real energizer. Sometimes if I am lacking a bit of confidence and need energizing, I use this mantra and repeat the powerful words to myself in my mind until I really start to believe it. When I am out running and reach the peak of a hill, I jump up and down and repeat the mantra to myself. It works, try it and see for yourself.

You can also use simple words like 'calm' and 'peace' - 'I am calm', 'I am peaceful'. These are wonderful especially if you suffer from anxiety. Say these words on your breath, and even try and breathe in calm and breathe out peace allowing your breath to flow.

Discover Chanting Mantras

I signed up for a two-year course to become a Life Celebrant with the One Spirit Interfaith Foundation in October 2012. On the course, we immersed ourselves in numerous religions, one per month. It was wonderful to extract the jewels out of each.

The first religion we covered was Hinduism which uses the sacred text called Sanskrit and has hundreds of mantras dedicated to so many subjects.

My first experience of chanting mantras was to learn the Gayatri mantra. The explanation that our teacher, gave to it was: 'This earthly being calls up on the heavens and beyond (invocation), connect to my essence as I transform light, love and peace. Blessed Be.' As she explained it, she performed a body prayer. This really connected with me. Holding her hands up high and looking up as if calling to a higher source of power. It was beautiful to watch.

The Gayatri Mantra:

> Om Bhur Bhuvaḥ Swaḥ Tat Savitur Vareñyaṃ Bhargo Devasya Dhīmahi
> Dhiyo Yo Naḥ Pracho Dayāteh

On the Sunday night, following my first weekend on the course, I called in to see my first-born beautiful daughter, who was living in London. While I was there, she asked me what I had learned. I shared my news with her, and she asked me to teach her the Gayatri Mantra. So, I did and to our surprise her Brazilian lodger also knew the mantra, so we sang it all together in her temple (we call it a temple, it's actually a conservatory with a beautiful big buddha within it). This was a beautiful memory I will treasure always.

Chapter 10: How to Calm Your Mind with Mantras

My second-born daughter, a fully trained yoga teacher, now knows this mantra plus many more. It's no surprise that we have adopted the Gayatri Mantra to become our family mantra.

Deva Premal and Mitten are well known for introducing Sanskrit mantras into the mainstream, they created a 21-day Mantra Meditation Challenge which can be downloaded from iTunes. We highly recommend this to anyone seeking a more spiritual understanding of themselves and the joys of mantras.

Lionel and I did this challenge on our trip to India. Oh, wow, chanting mantras together early in the morning as a couple was so special. It brings bliss into your very being. The bliss is in the silence following your chant.

Thank you to Deva Premal and Mitten for inspiring me to continue chanting the sacred mantras. I now chant every day as part of my morning spiritual practice. I strongly suggest you try it as part of your journey of discovery.

I love doing them so much that I set up a group called Tantra Mantra Tuesdays. Many friends come together at 7.00am just to chant, this is so powerful and uplifting when you are in a circle.

Lionel has two long chants which he does a set number of times within his early morning practice. He says it focusses the intentions he puts into every chakra and works on the nervous system to make him more happy, powerful, and connected.

Chapter 11
How to Discover Inner Happiness with Chanting

Another one of my favourite mantras is also a favourite of the Dalai Lama's. It's called 'Lokah Samastah Sukhino Bhavantu' and it translates to:

"May all beings be happy. May my thoughts, words and actions in some way contribute to the happiness of all beings."

Feel it, feel the feeling that everyone will benefit from our lives. It's so wonderful to know that we can make everyone around us happy.

It's a great thing making people happy, contemplating, and creating our own happiness is another matter. Many of the spiritual gurus when they talk of it, say happiness is a huge issue for most people. Happiness on one level looks very superficial. It's not easy to be truly happy, it is something that we need to contemplate.

To me, happiness is a childlike feeling of innocence in which we are just happy for no reason at all. Once we find this childlike innocence, where we are just happy for no reason at all, it can be accessed at any time.

I remember having just landed at a transfer airport. On the plane was a family with a nine-month-old baby. Oh, how I connected with the spirit of that baby. I was pulling faces, making baby noises, squeaking in baby talk, and making constant connection with the baby's eyes, it was pure magic.

I had a joyous connection and chatted happily and gave gratitude to the hostesses who served us. I was travelling alone but I was just so happy.

When we landed, I walked with my fellow passengers through the airport. On arriving in the superficial world of 'Duty Free' I was greeted by designer labels and expensive leather brands. The environment reminded me of animal cruelty, I felt the toxic air of perfume and saw rows and rows of disease inducing chocolates. Thousands of people are always seeking happiness through these products that cause devastation to this beautiful planet. How can these material things bring happiness? Their novelty is so short lived.

To make this world a happier place, we must start with ourselves.

Singing and chanting mantras is one way to reach happiness through which we can attain a state of contentment. Especially chanting the mantra, Lokah Samastah Sukhino Bhavantu.

We can nourish our thoughts to go in a positive direction, or we can let them slip into negativity which they can very easily do. Choose nourishment.

In this mantra is the Sanskrit word 'Bav' which means Devotional Divinity which makes us happy. So, it is important for us to be conscious, if we are conscious and present, we live in the Bav. To live in a way that increases our Bav, not decrease it, we need to focus on Bav Boosters not Bav Busters.

We instinctively know what these boosters and busters are. We know the feeling when we are being nourished. We know the feeling when something leaves us feeling empty.

Happiness is about choosing the things that lift our spirits, choosing things that make us more generous and more loving, towards ourselves and others.

Chapter 11: How to Discover Inner Happiness with Chanting

As we tune into ourselves more and more, we begin to realize what nourishes us and what is nourishing and beneficial to everyone around us.

Hosting Tantra Mantra Tuesday chanting mornings was magical. We appointed our very own Songbird, a beautiful singer and songwriter, to commence our session with her angelic voice. The mantra we always sang to start the session was Lokah Samastah Sukhino Bhavantu.

The mantra is about making all things happy, not just people, it's animals, insects, reptiles and all the living things around us. When you sing a mantra really focus on it and feel the vibration of happiness and the energy flowing through it.

Please be aware of your mind easily straying to other thoughts and bring your mind back to the words of the mantra. You will find that happiness, contentment, peace, and transformation are available from these sacred chants if you persist.

Mantras are like tuning forks; they tune our vibration to specific frequencies. Here are some examples of the frequencies:

Frequency / Vibration	Mantra
Happiness	Lokah Samastah Sukhino Bhavantu
Healing	Om Shree Dhanvantre Namaha
Abundance	Om Shree Maha Laxmi Namaha
New Beginnings	Om gum Ganapataye Namaha
Love	Aha Premal

BELIEVE IN LOVE

Peace   Om Shanti

Harmony   Om Bhur Bhuvah Swah etc. the Gyatri Mantra

We highly recommend Mantra Chanting CD's by Deva Premal and Mitten. www.devapremalmiten.com

Chapter 12
How to Connect with Nature

We cannot emphasize enough the importance of you spending time in nature, consciously connecting. Go for walks, notice the seasons, what is happening and changing all around you. Notice the activity in nature, the circles of life, the abundance of life, the natural flow of life.

I believe it is important to find your own nature, your soul's nature. This will be one of five elements in your soul reading, and this will determine what makes your soul sing. What element in nature really nourishes and nurtures your soul? For me, I'm a six-metal soul so I am nourished by earth. I love mountains, stone circles, rock outcrops and sandy beaches where I can run barefoot.

It is important for me to ground myself regularly on the earth. The elements here are the same as Chinese medicine elements, and the elements used in ancient Tibet, and of course in the wonderful eastern art of Feng Shui.

I suggest you discover your Soul Tribe, as I've talked about earlier in this book to discover your soul purpose number. This will reveal your specific soul nature, your soul's element, enabling you to find out what nurtures your soul or spirit.

Your soul element is one of five elements: Water (1) nurtures

- Wood (3,4)

Wood (3,4) nurtures – Fire (9)

Fire (9) nurtures – Earth (2,5.8)

Earth (2,5,8) Nurtures – Metal (6,7)

BELIEVE IN LOVE

Metal (6,7) nurtures – Water (1) And the cycle continues...

Once you know your Soul Tribe, you can find your soul's

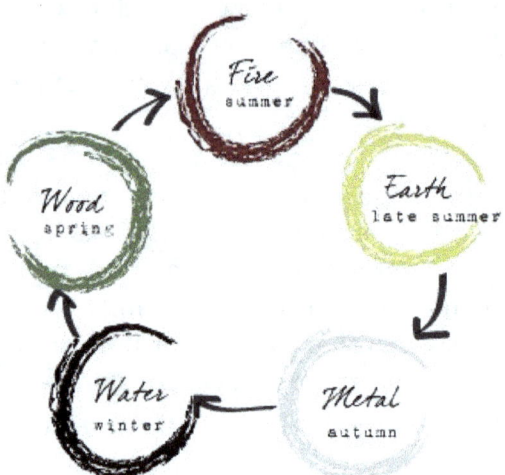

element and you will know what type of natural environment soothes and nurtures your soul.

1	= **Water** Being close to rivers, lakes and the ocean.
3 or 4	= **Wood** Being in woodlands, forests and jungles.
9	= **Fire** Being in hot tropical, sunny climates.
2, 5 or 8	= **Earth** Being barefoot on the beach or walking up mountains, visiting stone circles etc.
6 or 7	= **Metal** Similar to earth as earth nurtures metal. You will also love round shapes: round buildings, big silver balls and round objects as they nurture your soul too.

Find your favourite place in nature and ensure you visit it regularly.

Chapter 13
How to Experience Tantra

Bali has fascinated me since my first visit. I have visited Bali on many occasions and usually always do an annual detox at a health retreat. Each time I go I visit so many temples and always go back to Batukaru.

In 2003, I was recommended to have a massage by Ketut Asana at his Body Works Centre on Hanuman Street in Ubud. I noticed in a leaflet that he had a weekly Puja ceremony at his ashram called The Kundalini Tantra Ashram. I am now a Puja junkie. I always want to be blessed and sprinkled with holy water. I went each Tuesday to get my blessing fix.

To get to the main area of the ceremony you had to give offering to approximately eight different altars or shrines. One being a fresh spring where you cleansed yourself with the happy water. Here you would drink three times, splash the water on your forehead three times and then splash over the top of your head three times. It was so refreshing and awakening. It made me feel alive.

Everyone gathered in the ceremonial hall which was adjacent to a large carving of a Shiva Lingam.

When Ketut Asana arrived, we started our chants. He blessed us all and we danced around the Shiva Lingam continuing with our chanting. This is where I first experienced pure unconditional bliss throughout my body. I felt as if I was connected to the whole universe as one. In harmony, being held.

My body started to tingle, and I felt at one with all and then from the base of my spine to the top of my head came the most incredible flow of out of this world tingling. Pulsating, flowing, growing, glowing, inner ecstasy, it filled me with divine energy.

Everyone at the Puja was Balinese so there was no one I could share my experience with or ask advice from. I just accepted and enjoyed it and went home with a twinkle and a tingle. I was mystified by my experience.

So, my message to you here is to follow your intuition; mine was to go to temples and explore the spirit of Bali and it led me to a purely blissful, ecstatic experience. Years later when I have described my experience to more spiritual people, they have told me, 'Oh Dawn, you were experiencing a Kundalini Rising.'

So began my understanding that there was more out there than just physical sex for a fulfilling experience, and then when I met my Tantric Guru Sex God Soul mate Lionel, he taught me the rest.

Chapter 14
How to Nurture Your Spirit

This is a big one, you need to think back to when you were a child, what did you love to do? So many times, as we grow, we disconnect from that childlike spirit inside us that wants to be nurtured.

Put some calming instrumental music on, sit quietly and dream about your childhood. Really think about anything you remember about being creative. If writing is not your forte, then imagine a picture of you as a child. Was it drawing, painting, making things, cooking with Mum, woodwork with Dad, walking in nature, going for wild swims, paddling in rivers, making sandcastles, or burying each other in the sand, cycling, skipping, dancing, singing, or sewing perhaps?

Write or draw your memories:

As for me, I grew up in the Cheshire countryside exploring in the woods, collecting bundles of wild-flowers for my mum. Making dens in the forest, exploring bluebell woods, playing in the River Dane, floating down the river on giant blow up chairs with my friends. I loved making things. I remember making a go cart from my old pram and a rabbit run from old pallets, to allow my bunny to have fresh grass.

I was so lucky to have my own pony too, she was called Sindy Lu and I loved creating colourful jumping poles. I loved caring for her; getting up at 5am every morning before school and looking after her, she was my best friend. Being out in nature, just Sindy Lu and I, are some of my most precious memories.

My mum taught me to sew at an early age, so my other passion was making clothes, especially for my Sindy doll. My dolls were the best dressed, most stylish dolls in the world...well, in my world anyway.

This later developed into designing and making my own clothes or modifying the clothes I bought. I bought my first wedding dress for £80 from Pronuptia, it was an off the shoulder dress. I removed one of the sleeves and transformed it into a one shoulder dress. I sewed on feathers, pearls, and diamanté. Wow was it spectacular, especially the plume I put on my head dress. I loved it; it was my own creation.

Even when I was very little, I couldn't stop sketching. I started with just a pencil, later I developed a love for sketching in charcoal and pastel. I'd spend hours sketching pictures of my dog and of nature, focusing on what I was putting on the paper. My most impressive piece of art was of Bob Marley when I was 18. I loved his spirit.

So, what are you doing now to nurture your spirit?

My spirit nurturing now comes from getting out in nature either by myself or with the company of my beautiful man, or my grandchildren. My favourite place in nature is called the Bosley Cloud, just a mile away from my hometown. I always go to the peak of the Cloud and empower myself through the freedom to wail if I am upset about anything. When I am on top of Cloud Mountain (that is what my Granddaughter calls it) it feels as if I am conversing with Mother Earth. It's as if she holds me in her arms like a little girl and allows me to cry.

Two major ley lines kiss on the top of Cloud Mountain. They are the Spine of Albion; Ellen the female serpent ley line, and Belinus the male serpent ley line. If you take your divining rods up to the top of The Cloud, you will be able to find the two ley lines and discover the kissing point where they cross. I love to sit and dream on this kissing point, to find balance and harmony, blending the feminine goddess energy of Ellen with

Chapter 14: How to Nurture Your Spirit

the masculine warrior energy of Belinus.

As my soul nature element is metal, I am nourished and nurtured by earth. On the backbone of Cloud Mountain there are some neolithic megaliths, called The Bridgestone's. In ancient times, the Bridgestone's were a big stone circle, larger than Stonehenge, sadly only a few stones remain. Sometimes I go there and lie down on one of the rocks. I simply wait, listen, and enjoy.

Between the years of 1995 and 2010 we had four dogs: Molly, Simba, Titch and Tiny. Molly was an Old English sheepdog, I called Simba a Pharaoh dog as she had such big ears, she was an Alsatian cross, Tiny was a white miniature shaggy poodle and Titch a black miniature poodle. For those blissful fifteen years I was running in nature with my little tribe.

Nature is my biggest contentment and happiness bringer, so much so that I chose my house because it had a blue bell wood, ancient forest, silver birch woodland and meadows to nurture my spirit into my mature years.

When you are able to nurture your spirit and understand your connection with something bigger than yourself, you are able to align and find balance within. Everyday events make us out of balance and only when we are able to nurture our spirit frequently, are we able to be at one with the world and live in the moment.

Be adventurous. Try new things. Try things that challenge you.

Healing back pain in just five minutes: A few years ago, I developed a serious lower back pain. It hurt so much that even the simplest of tasks such as cleaning my teeth were agonizing. I met a gentleman called Chris Payne at a networking event. I mentioned about my pain as his surname prompted me. He told me about a healing disc that would heal my back. Rubbish I thought at first, how could a disc cure me? But then I reminded myself to open my mind to new ideas and researched this disc.

It was called the Empower Disc, to me it looked like a computer healing programme. I called and made an appointment with Russell Treasure to tell me more about the disc, he came to meet Lionel and I in the barn at Blissland.

He sat down and explained about the Empower Disc. It sounded just too good to be true. So, of course, I gave it a go. Lionel videoed me while I was experiencing the healing. Russell gave me a small purple aluminium disc to hold with my both of my hands. He said look at the disc, feel it and connect with it. I followed his instructions and began to rock backwards and forwards. He then asked me to put the disc in my right hand loosely, and to be very conscious and aware of the pain in my back.

He asked me to say: "Give me what I need and remove the pain and the source of the pain in my back at the fastest possible speed starting now ... Go." Well, what happened after that simply shocked and amazed Lionel and me. I started to sway and gyrate my hips. I went up and down on my tip toes. I danced and swirled about, up, and down. Then it all stopped around five minutes later. Russell asked me if the pain was still there. Guess what? The pain had gone, and it never came back.

We were intrigued and bought a disc. Lionel and I attended several courses with the incredible creator of the Empower Disc, Coby Zvikler to utilize the disc to its full potential. What an amazing discovery.

Chapter 14: How to Nurture Your Spirit

Whatever the reasoning behind the power of the disc or the suggestion of the healing, the fact is that if I hadn't been open to trying new things, alternative things or looking at things with an open mind, I may well have suffered for much longer or gone through a much more complicated and expensive procedure to arrive at the same healing.

We are firm believers in there being many alternative healings for all sorts of health issues, and that most ill health is a consequence of what we eat and the environment we are in.

We always refer to our alternative health bible called Alternative Cures by Bill Gottlieb at the first symptom of any ailment.

By being open to all things and trying different ways of achieving results, you allow the adventurous child in you to be healed too.

Past life regression

Sounds scary. It is, or it can be. I went to a retreat called Kamalaya in Thailand in 2011 with my two daughters for a wonderful detox. The retreat had incredibly powerful visiting practitioners.

Mark Beal was the name of the past life regression therapist. I was intrigued so I booked on. Mark started the process by taking me to a trance like state. Lying down on my back I was transported in my dream that seemed like reality. I was an Amazonian healer who lived in the mountains in South America. I lived on the top of the mountain with a group of healers. We were outcasts of the village lower down the mountain. I heard voices and noise coming from down the mountain side. Fires started to burn on top of our mountain.

A warrior from the village speared me with a wooden spear through my heart. As I was dying and burning in the fire, I saw someone kill the warrior who killed me.

I was covered with sweat and screaming out loud in the room with my husband. It was as if I had been killed, I experienced it all so vividly. During the session my husband revealed to me that my younger daughter in this life, was the elder wise woman in the village below. The warrior who killed me was my husband and my fellow healer who killed him was my oldest daughter. Well, I kept this quiet for many years as it was so unbelievable.

I went back through other past lives too during my time there. The second time I was entwined in white light with another ethereal being experiencing pure bliss. The third time I was an Indian princess who had fallen in love with a poor boy and secretly seeing him against my mum's and dad's, the king's, and queen's, wishes.

The fourth time I was a wayward woman with large breasts in the Middle Ages. Wow! what a wicked experience – she was living a wild life!

I can now relate to all my past life experiences in this life. And each one has touched me and taught me lessons which bring more clarity to this life.

Nourish your spirit

Retreat from your everyday life and treat yourself. Yep, I have done this many times and recommend it.

Kamalaya in Koh Samui was a special one, it was built around a monk's cave. Every tree and rock were preserved in the

Chapter 14: How to Nurture Your Spirit

construction. Whilst I was there, I was fascinated by the Monks' Cave. I took solace there every day and would light a candle and incense and just sit alone, retreating from the world into Mother Earth.

I found it so peaceful and nurturing. The energy in there was so special.

Another retreat my two daughters and I went to was the Ubud Sari in Bali. Here we followed a juice fast programme. We did yoga and meditation every day and participated in many massages and colonic cleanses.

Wow, we found them all so nourishing for our mind, body, and soul.

Unconditional loving relationship

The best nurturing of my spirit is my love affair with my twin flame, soul mate, lover, and best friend Lionel. My forever-man. The days and nights we spend alone together send me to heavenly bliss.

We have no expectations of each other, there is a freedom between us that also bonds us in the most beautiful conscious tantric way.

When we are together and connected, I feel a sense of bliss. Every moment we are together I look at him and cannot believe how this beautiful human being has fallen in love with me.

The way he dresses, especially in his yoga gear, bright orange, and turquoise linen. All the clothes he wears, he buys for their eco-friendliness and their tactility. So, he feels beautiful too. His words are so generous and kind to all. His silence is golden beams of light shining from his heart. He is a very special man.

Do you have a partner? If so, take the time in your life to write down in the space here all the beauty you see in him or her. Use it as a meditation, or message of thanks or appreciation to indirectly receive more blessings. Add to it on additional pages if you can.

Chapter 15
How to Transform Darkness to Light

Expose your inner darkness, accept it, and forgive yourself.

I am writing this part of the book whilst on a flight back to Manchester having been away on my own. I had reached the point of exhaustion at home, I was the heaviest weight I'd ever been, and my happiness factor was low. I was lethargic and completely out of balance. I knew what I needed to do, yeah you know it too. Retreat.

My soul mate, Lionel, took charge of all my caring duties and the causes of my stress (mostly regarding my mother) back home and I disappeared to Bali, my spiritual home to indulge in a 21-day Panchakarma Ayurveda healing retreat at Amtra Siddhi in Nyuh Kuning Ubud run by the most amazing doctor, Dr Sujatha.

The Ayuvedic healing was wonderful, the retreat was so peaceful and the accommodation incredible. I knew I had more work to do than just the physical, so I had some emotional Soulful Theta Healing Sessions with Dr Sujatha too. She convinced me of the following:

1. I have a right to be happy. I can say no. I don't have to please everyone all the time. I am worthy, I can do as I please. My first session was releasing the guilt of always having to please everyone and not feeling worthy.

2. Money – I felt stuck. Dr Sujatha asked me about my childhood and if I had been criticized. I explained about my head teacher at the grammar school who told me I was not intelligent enough to be a vet, when I expressed an interest in the profession. Dr Sujatha also extracted much of the criticism I had experienced from my ex-

husband, she put me into a peaceful place and asked me to put my hand on my heart and repeat affirmations while she held my other hand and connected to my body's psyche. She asked me to repeat after her, "I am clever."

Pow! This made tears burst out of my eyes and my stomach wrench in sadness. I'm sure it was my body releasing the pain I experienced for 45 years of not being thought of as clever, or certainly not being told so.
She then continued for me to repeat these words:

> I believe in myself
> I trust myself
> I allow myself to earn money
> I am responsible
> I am responsible with money
> My services are valuable
> My skills are respected

And then she got me to say, "I release all negative messages and energies from my past relationship."

Dr Sujatha did a magical job on healing; it was painful but professionally and profoundly well done with such love.

The Panchakarma 21-day retreat helped me lose 8 kg/17 lbs in weight. People at the retreat noticed and commented, "Wow! You look stunning, you are glowing Dr Dawn."

I felt so privileged at being called Dr Dawn by all the team at Amrta Siddhi. This made me feel so special. One guest asked what my Doctorate was for, and I said, "I'm the Doctor of Happiness,". She responded by saying, "You are Dr Dawn, the Spirit Doctor as you are so passionate, you inspire everyone's spirit that you meet."

Chapter 15: How to Transform Darkness to Light

I did lots of my Feng Shui Astrology readings at the retreat, if I met anyone born in the northern hemisphere, I'd jump on them and give them guidance on their Soul Purpose, Emotional Passion, and Physical Power. Also, whilst there, I spent time with another guest, a lady with cancer and discovered that her issue was really her own mind. I noticed how she spoke to the therapists. How she ordered them around as if she was superior to them. No please or thank you ever left her lips.

So, I slapped her on the arm and told her off. I explained how gratitude and appreciation is the source of love. Please show your helpers' love by saying please and thank you. She pointed at her throat and just whispered, "I can't as I can't speak". I showed her the hand gesture of putting her hands in the prayer position on her heart. A beautiful gesture of gratitude to share with those around her. I also asked her about her morning routines and if she had any spiritual practice to support her on her journey to wellness. 'No', she replied. I shared with her my morning ritual song which I perform with Lionel when we are at home together.

Morning Ritual Song:
Every little cell in my body is happy
Every little cell in my body is well
Every little cell in my body is happy
Every little cell in my body is well
I'm so glad every little cell, every little cell in my body is well
I'm so glad every little cell, every little cell in my body is well.

I also shared about how singing mantras can help soothe and calm her busy mind. I made her videos of:
1. Every Little Cell Song
2. Happiness Mantra – Lokah Samasta Sukhino Bhavantu
3. Unblocking Obstacles song - Om Gum Ganapataye Namaha.
4. Healing Mantra - Om shree Dhanvantre Namaha.

Oh, wow, she loved them. The other thing she needed was help finding a companion carer. She lived alone in Sanur Bali on the beach. I told her all about the amazing companion carer we had found for my mum, and I agreed to help her do a job specification so she could advertise for one.

Dr. Sujatha heard about me helping her and so many others and reminded me that I was on this retreat to nurture myself not others. That's a toughie when it's in your nature to help and support others.

I made a note of what she had said and stopped jumping on people. I decided to take some quiet time alone, writing and reflecting.

I also felt I wanted more release, particularly after feeling how my ex-husband had influenced my lack of confidence in later life, so I went to the healing centre at the Yoga Barn in Ubud. Here I was drawn to two healers:

1. Psychic Surgery with Punu
2. Cranio Sacral Therapy with Adolph

Psychic Surgery with Punu

I believe in following your intuition. Punu's picture emitted a beautiful authentic energy. So, at 10.00am on the 12th April 2019 I had Psychic Surgery.

Punu prepared his altar and made his little healing hut by the river into a place of sacred pure energy. We sat down, and he asked me why I was there and what was my objective for our session. I was very clear, I wanted to psychically remove any Karmic attachments or energy from my ex-husband that was holding me back. He went silent and told me that we must not blame anyone else for how we are or how we feel. It is up to

Chapter 15: How to Transform Darkness to Light

us to release these feelings. I must do it myself.

He put a chair in the middle of the room and asked me to sit on it which I did. He asked me to close my eyes and he put on beautiful music. I sensed him circling me and I know he was calling in his helpers from the higher realms. He asked me to speak out loud and communicate clearly to all the people who had hurt me in my life.

To speak to them directly as if they were present with us. Wow, so many came out.

Oh my, the pain and rage that emotionally came from within me. The pain in my stomach and womb was intense, I felt as if I was being stabbed.

Punu told me to calm myself and asked what colours and shapes I was seeing. I could see a red triangle with a violet star on the top of it point (I had no ideas of its relevance). He then asked me to speak out loud again and forgive all these people and ask for forgiveness for all the people I had hurt in my life. The tears flooded and flooded. I had so many people to say sorry to and so much hurt to forgive.

Over the space of a lifetime so much emotional pain happens to us and we create so much pain for others.

When you lay it out before you and realize how you have affected others and been affected by others, it takes some serious work to remove the emotional chains. Oh, how I cried and cried, releasing all my sorrow and sadness.

Punu guided me through. Forgiveness was the key.

When I'd released all my pain, Punu put some beautiful music on and allowed peace and silence to arrive before I opened my eyes. We moved by the window to the therapist's chairs, and I drank lots of water. I could not say thank you enough to Punu.

Punu said to me that my older daughter is my guide, "Dawn, she is your Angel – listen to her and what she suggests. She knows what you need to become whole."

If ever you get change to visit Punu at the Yoga Barn, Ubud in Bali, please do.

Cranio Sacral Therapy with Adolph

Cranio Sacral Therapy with Adolf was fascinating. Adolph asked me why I was there, so I told him about my tinnitus. He said he could not heal me; he had not had success in the past so I asked him what he could do. He told me Cranio Sacral Therapy was about balancing the skeletal structure and meridians of energy in the body. He also stated he was an advanced kinesiologist and said he could test my organs.

Following his explanation, he instructed me to lie down on the bed so he could do some muscle testing in my stomach area. He said I had a slight infection in my kidneys and that Colloidal Silver was the cure, just five teaspoonfuls a day.

He advised me to go to see my doctor back home and ask for my blood sugars and urine to be tested. I think this was to prove to me that what he was saying was right. His advice to me was to completely cut out refined sugar. It was not good for me. Low sugar from natural fruits are fine but I should avoid anything else.

Simply amazing. He was able to detect problems and give me the cures without any symptoms manifesting themselves into

Chapter 15: How to Transform Darkness to Light

a real illness.

The more we trust alternative methods to detect problems before they become serious, the healthier we'll be.

I loved his Cranio Sacral therapy. When he touched the back of my head and my skull, I could feel energy flowing and moving all around my body, it was just astonishing.

I highly recommend Adolph at the Yoga Barn, Ubud in Bali.

Chapter 16
How to Find Your Soul Tribe

Feng Shui Tribe

From 2011 I have had and still have the most beautiful soulful, spiritual connection with five gorgeous women with whom I studied Feng Shui. They are Olga, Natasha, Alkistis, Stella and Frederique.

Oh, how in alignment we are in our thinking and our belief systems! We allow each other to just be or come together to have ceremonies, healing, rituals and more. Bless their souls for crowning me a wise woman on my 60th birthday. Oh wow, the messages were profoundly moving and the ceremony magical.

These beautiful women are truly my soul tribe.

Soul Sister

During 2012 to 2014 I did a two-year One Spirit Interfaith Foundation Ministry Course and was ordained as a Reverend in my legal name. I thought I would have developed a spiritual soul tribe from all the people on a similar journey but the only person who I deeply felt a soul connection with is a person I introduced to the course, and that is my friend Deana Stone. She is another soul sister of mine.

During one of my retreats, I connected with a lady called Delores, I could feel her spiritual and soulful beauty. Delores is a goddess in her own right. Some folks I meet on retreats eat meat, drink alcohol, they are not living consciously, and many of the people I met were burnt out yoga teachers – now that's strange!

What I am saying here is that you need to develop a soul tribe that truly resonates with you. Take your time finding your soul tribe and once again go on adventures and on a voyage of discovery.

Let your vibe attract your tribe.

Women's Circles

My daughter joined a women's circle at the Yoga Barn on her last visit to Ubud, Bali. And when she knew, I was going to Bali she said, 'Oh mum you must go.' I couldn't wait!

Wow! 50 women in a circle or I should say 50 beautiful goddesses. A wonderful lady hosted the circle. The structure went like this:

1. The host opened the space, and we invited our ancestors and other women in our lives, alive or in heaven, to join us in the circle.
2. The host gave us an overview of what will happen and set boundaries of time and communication.
3. The host gave us the subject for the circle.
4. We were given a piece of paper and a pen to scribble notes on the chosen subject and to write down how we felt about it.
5. We divined a card to guide us.
6. The host passed a talking stick around the circle and one by one each woman shared their story.
7. On finishing we had a short open circle and debate about the subject.
8. The circle was closed with a blessing and prayer and sincere gratitude.

Chapter 16: How to Find Your Soul Tribe

Feng Shui Tribe

As you can imagine the Yoga Barn in Ubud attracts very lean Yogic goddesses, mainly around the ages of 23 – 40. I was the eldest there.

The circle's subject that night was breasts. That's right, breasts. We were going to discuss our bodies.

Breasts

Out of the 50 women present, there were only two of us who felt positive about and adored our own breasts. Most other women had issues; too small, too big, a complete lack of love and respect for their beautiful feminine selves. Unbelievable.

One big message for all you beautiful women out there reading this book is to massage your breasts every day: a key learning from the circle. As our breasts are so wrapped up in bras and yoga tops all day, they need to move to allow our lymph system to flow. We discussed and agreed on the importance of not wearing bras. To let our breasts, hang free and bounce so that the movement helps our lymphatic draining system flow better. Great advice – and it's free to do!

And please, if you do wear bras, do not wear under-wired ones. In this electronic world the under-wire acts as a radio antenna and attracts electromagnetic waves from electrical equipment which affect our cells adjacent to these wires. So please, please choose alternative non-conductive bras to wear, and please buy natural fabrics too.

I asked my daughter what the subject was when she went to the Women's circle, and she explained 'Orgasms'. Oh, la la! I'm sorry I missed that one, it would have been very revealing.

Whilst out in Bali earlier in 2019 I attended two women's circles at the Yoga Barn held at the River Dome adjacent to the flowing water. They were of a similar structure to the one I attended before, but these were hosted by a different lady called Nadine. The subjects were very different too.

The first circle subject was leadership. Most of the women spoke about how they were lost and wanted to find their true purpose and authentic self. I would say that 80% of the women in the circle had come to Bali to find themselves. Attractive, young, and beautiful yet lost women, most with deep relationship issues. This was a real eye opener for me.

The second circle subject was grief. Once again, most women were grieving relationship break ups, grieving their childhood and upbringing, and wanting to move into a new life. Some women were also grieving how they always attracted abusive partners and needed to free themselves of this and find true unconditional love.

Women's voices need to be heard

We need these safe women's circles all over the world, they are a beautiful way of allowing women's voices to be heard. All you need for a soulful authentic woman circle is a leader to set rules, boundaries, timings, structure, a subject to discuss and a beautiful sacred space for the event to be held in. It can be a very rewarding experience for everyone.

Lionel hosts a monthly men's circle and has done for several years. Whilst I don't get to hear much about what goes on, I imagine it to be very similar, giving men the opportunity to talk openly to each other. What I do hear about it, is the value the men get from it and the importance the men put on it for their own understanding of life.

Chapter 16: How to Find Your Soul Tribe

Feng Shui Tribe

Whilst in Bali, I kept visioning a big round wooden building where we live. I could see a Goddess temple to honour women. A place where many women circles can be held as well as so many more women related rituals. Yes, it will be open to men to come in and honour the goddess, goddesses of the season, goddesses in their own lives and light a candle for them on the main altar.

This is just one of the projects I will be working towards after completing and publishing this book. I'm so excited!

On the subject of women, I personally honour the Dalai Lama's statement. "The World will be saved by the western woman."

Oh, how I believe this statement. Just recently I've been dreaming of creating a community of women online and in person, where our voices can be heard, and we can share our projects and activities. A space where we can share what we are doing to empower women and children and how we are making a difference and creating a better world.

What is a better world? I'll leave you to put your own interpretation on that. I believe anything we can do to help the collective consciousness must be positive. Women are becoming more powerful in their own right. Many of us still need to realize it though and help bring about the changes needed.

Chapter 17
How to Balance Your Mind, Body, and Soul with Ayurveda

Ayurveda healthy living.

After only experiencing a 21-day Panchakarma Healing, I am not an expert like Dr Sujatha or Dr Remil at the Amtra Siddhi Ayurveda healing centre. All I can tell you is I highly recommend you finding out what your body type is and following a diet plan.

The three body types are:

Vata = Air and Space Pitta = Fire and Water Kapha = Earth and Water

Each of us has a very different body composition and digestive needs.

Basically, the thinking is, if you don't follow your body type or listen to the signs in your body where you are becoming out of balance, you will become poorly.

Here is a simple overview of the three body types do's and don'ts.

"If your body and mind were a hand-written story, then vata is the ink, pitta is the pen, and kapha is the paper. Each one is vital." – Kaitlin Lacey

	VATA	PITTA	KAPHA
"Spirit Symbol"	Air	Fire	Earth
Common traits:	Dry, Light, Cold	Oily, Hot, Light	Heavy, Slow, Cold
Work type:	Type A	Mostly Type A	Type B
Comforting foods:	Astringent Bitter	Sour Pungent	Sweet Salty

Chapter 17: How to Balance Your Mind, Body, and Soul with Ayurveda

Balanced when:	Clear perspective Creative Artistic	Discernment Sharp memory Joyful	Gentle Emotionally in-tune Strong endurance
Imbalanced when:	Anxious Spacey Moody Insomnia Stiff muscles	Judgmental Angry Controlling Inflammation breakouts Hot flashes Skin rashes Diarrhoea	Fearful of letting go Set in ways Depression Obesity Congestion Excessive sleep Irregular bowel
Triggers for imbalance:	Not being true to oneself Eating on the run Spreading self too thin	Overworking Eating while angry Overheating activity (workouts)	Sedentary lifestyle Emotional eating Storing of emotions

Vata Balancing Dietary Advice

AVOID:	- Generally: - Cold, raw and dry foods, carbonated or cold drinks - Spicy, pungent, overly bitter or astringent tastes - All sour and unripe fruits - White sugar and yeast - Skipping meals, late nights, excessive stimulation
Introduce:	- Rhythm to your life (waking and sleeping times, rest periods) - Meditation, Tai Chi or Yoga - Regular mealtimes: more frequent meals, less amount - Watch and control mental tendencies of worry and fear - Daily self-massage with oil (cold climate use sesame oil, hot climate coconut oil) - Soothing calming music

Vata Balancing Foods

Grains	Rice (including wild rice, quinoa, oats wheat)
Pules:	Mung beans, mung dahl
Vegetables:	Squash, beetroot, carrots, coriander, parsnip, peas, cucumber, leeks, okra, pumpkin, olives, asparagus, sweet potatoes, zucchini.
Fruits:	Most sweet fruit, apples cooked, avocados, apricots, lemon and lime, bananas, coconuts, cherries, fresh dates, and figs, soaked raisins, grapes, strawberries, berries

	(except cranberries) pears, mangoes
Nuts:	Okay in moderation, peel skin off almonds
Seeds:	Pumpkin, sesame, sunflower, tahini, flax
Condiments:	All except chocolate, pepper, and sprouts in moderation
Oils:	Cooking: sesame, olive External use: avocado, sesame and in summer, coconut
Drinks:	Juices see fruits and vegetables, chai, almond milk, teas - chamomile, elderflower, fresh ginger, eucalyptus, lemon grass, lavender, liquorice, peppermint and spearmint, rose-hip, saffron, fennel
Spices:	All fine to use

Pitta Balancing Dietary Advice

AVOID:	-Generally: sour, salty, and pungent foods -Oily and deep-fried foods -Alcohol and coffee -Exposure to hot sun (sunbathing) -Watch feelings of anger, hate and intensity
Introduce:	-Sweet, astringent, and bitter tastes -Pleasant and cooling activities to your life like walks in nature -Tai Chi and meditation - A warm and caring and nurturing and non-competitive attitude

Pitta Balancing Foods	
Grains:	Coconut, granola, oat bran, pasta, rice (not brown), spelt oats, wheat
Pulses:	Mung beans, mung dahl, chickpeas, kidney beans, red and brown lentils, split peas, black and white beans, tofu and tempeh, pinto beans, soya beans and other soy products (soya sauce in moderation)
Vegetables:	Preferably bitter and sweet: beetroot, broccoli, carrots, coriander, parsley, fennel, cucumber, asparagus, cauliflower, celery, zucchini, green beans, olives, artichokes, okra, kale, wheat grass, pumpkin, squash, parsnips, cooked onions, leafy greens, lettuce, peas, wheat grass, sweet potatoes, jack fruit (ripe)
Fruits:	Most sweet fruit, apples (cooked), avocados, pomegranate, apricots, pineapple, sweet oranges, bananas, coconuts, cherries, fresh dates, (used daily is good for calming pitta) figs, plums, raisins, mangoes, berries (except cranberries), melons, papaya, and lime (in moderation) Grapes of all types, draksha grapes are the best
Nuts:	Coconuts, almonds soaked and peeled
Seeds:	Pumpkin, sunflower, flax, popcorn, fennel seeds
Condiments:	Coriander, sweet mango chutney, sprouts, tamarind (in moderation)

Chapter 17: How to Balance Your Mind, Body, and Soul with Ayurveda

Oils:	Cooking: - canola, flax seed, olive, sunflower, walnut External: avocado, in summer coconut
Drinks:	Juices (see fruits and vegetables) Aloe vera juice, chai, almond milk, teas - chamomile, rose, fresh ginger, fennel, hibiscus, chicory, Jasmin, lemon grass, lavender, liquorice, peppermint and spearmint, nettle, dandelion, raspberry, saffron Sugarcane – it calms Pitta, it also cleanses kidney / bladder Rose – rose water, rose petals are excellent to calm Pitta, it is also helpful in reducing acidity. Cucumber juice – very cooling / also applied as face pack
Spices:	Coriander, cumin, fennel, mint, ginger fresh, basil, turmeric, saffron, peppermint, dill, cinnamon, parsley, and black pepper in moderation Neem leaves – chew neem leaves to calm Pitta and to improve food taste and skin

Kapha Balancing Dietary Advice

AVOID:	Generally: Cold, raw, oily, fried and other heavy foods - Sweet, sour, salty taste - Milk products - Eating after sunset - Overeating - Day sleeping - Dampness
Introduce:	- Regular exercise routines Limited sleep, waking early and rising at sunrise - Early and light dinners

Kapha Balancing Foods

Grains:	Basmati rice, wild rice, quinoa, dry oats, oat bran, polenta, millet, corn, barley, rye, couscous, buckwheat, seitan, granola, muesli, amaranth
Pulses:	Chickpeas, red and brown lentils, pinto beans, white beans, split peas, tempeh, tofu, mung beans, mung dahl
Vegetables:	Squash, beetroot, carrots, coriander, artichokes, brussel sprouts, turnips, peas, leeks, okra, pumpkin, asparagus, cauliflower, cabbage, celery, garlic, parsley, onions, spinach, carrots, kale, mustard greens, radishes, wheat grass, lettuce

Chapter 17: How to Balance Your Mind, Body, and Soul with Ayurveda

Fruits:	Most astringent fruits, apples, apricots, lemon and lime, cherries, pears, peaches, cranberries, dry figs, prunes, raisins, grapes, strawberries, pomegranates, berries
Nuts:	None
Seeds:	Pumpkin, sunflower, flax, popcorn - without oil or salt
Condiments	Black pepper, chilli pepper, spring onions, horseradish, spicy chutney, mustard, sprouts
Oils:	Cooking use little only – almond, canola, corn, sunflower: External: almond or sesame
Drinks:	Juices (see fruits and vegetables), chai, teas chamomile, ginger, cinnamon, lemongrass, fennel, clove, nettle, lavender, peppermint, and spearmint
Spices:	All fine to use except salt

BELIEVE IN LOVE

STEP 3 – Deepen:
Lionel takes you on a journey to help you make your dreams come true.

Dedication

Chapter 1 - Lionel's Perspective – Introducing Heart Freedom

Chapter 2 - Seven Steps to Success

Chapter 3 - Intentions and Objectives

Chapter 4 - Finding Love

Chapter 5 - Fear of Loss

Chapter 6 - Barriers

Chapter 7 - Motivation

Chapter 8 - Mind of Love

Chapter 9 - One True Love

Chapter 10 - To Love or Not to Love

Chapter 11 - Beliefs

Chapter 12 - Are you Worthy of Love

Chapter 13 - Seek Love

Chapter 14 - Your Own Love Beliefs

Chapter 15 - Learning to Love

Chapter 16 - Clear Yourself for Love

Chapter 17 - Let Love Flow

Chapter 18 - What Sort of Love do you Want

Chapter 19 - Your Love Type Chapter 20 - Know Thy Own Love

Chapter 21 - Building Heart Freedom

Chapter 22 – Creating Heart Freedom Conclusion

Dedication

"There are people that take from the world, and there are those who give to it. Everyone who knew my wife Dawn, knew her for the beautiful energy she exuded. Her heart was full of love, and she brought laughter wherever she went. Her beauty touched the spirit of many souls, and I am honoured to be one. Positivity ruled her life, beauty ruled her head and love ruled her heart. To find such a harmonic balance in one person is larger than life and that was Dawn. Her generosity was well known. Her passion was infectious. Her feelings were bold and caring. Dawn touched so many lives, in so many ways, mine more than most. To me she was Dawny Bird, the free spirit that soared above all others and swooped and danced and played in my love for her. She was a free spirit. My life with Dawn was full of colour, vibrancy and fun. Our energies entwined like twin flames. Our thoughts connected with twin understanding. Our hearts combined through twin spirits. I rejoice in Dawn revealing her divine journey.

Now she's in heaven she's bringing her light to us and shares all she learnt. Dawn loved change and knew change is the only constant in life. She'll be changing everything in heaven now, and her message in our hearts will live on through all those who knew her.

A Pueblo Indian Prayer I dedicate to my Dawny Bird: "Hold on to all that is good, even if it's just a handful of earth. Hold on to what you believe, even if it's a tree that stands alone. Hold on to what you must do, even if the journey is long and hard. Hold on to life and love, even when it's easier to let go. Hold on to my hand, even if I've gone away from you."

Confucius said that everything has beauty but not everyone sees it. Appreciate everything that the Divine gives us all, every day. I am so very grateful for every minute I spent with Dawn.

Dawny, I love you. I am so proud to share our story."

Lionel xxx

Chapter 1
Lionel's Perspective: *Introducing Heart Freedom*

I feel, hear, and see my own spiritual path as the most valuable thing in my life. It's been my saviour and continues to be my mainstay as I move into a headspace that will determine the legacy I leave; the respect, the appreciation, and the gratitude I will offer to the world in any emotional, physical and spiritual sense.

You can either be right or you can be happy. Why do so many of us choose to be unhappy by trying to be right? We are always our own worst enemies. Often the things we want to be right about aren't even important. Sometimes we perpetuate pain. What others think of you is not nearly as important as what you think of yourself.

One way I try to guide people to a better way of living is by helping them to establish a purpose and a passion for life. As young children we probably felt it without constraint. The instinctive, intuitive, innocence of childhood rarely lasts past seven years old, as we then let other people's actions, opinions and words have more meaning than our own.

Happiness is found through being appreciative of everything and grateful for everything. That includes the challenges and learning from the deeds of others. Emotional pain is passed on in many ways. A person is hurt by someone whose opinion about them they value in some way. That value may be completely misguided of course. They then can pass on that hurt, through their opinion of or attitude to others who value them in some way. Few people manage to sort out in adulthood what they instinctively knew in childhood.

I should perhaps at this juncture point out that earlier on in this book you may have understood me to have been having sexual relations with an inordinate number of women. I don't deny this, however it was not necessarily the philandering male spreading his wild seeds as it may appear to some. One thing I instinctively knew was that if Dawn was to judge me during our first telephone conversation, our relationship had no future. On the other hand, if Dawn was willing to accept or at least listen, I could intuit that we had something very powerful between us. Her return call on that notable afternoon said exactly that to me, even though her own interpretation may have been different, in the fullness of time she heard as well as accepted. She heard how each of the relationships had come about through major emotional traumas. How each of the women in their own way, received something from me that they valued whether in an emotional, physical, or spiritual context. My courses explain this more fully, and help people understand and value their relationships.

There was even an eighth relationship that tested my connection with Dawn and my correlation with myself to the nth degree. As we came to accept that we were indeed meant to be together, the other relationships fell away without drama. Only Dawn was able to offer me the connectedness of emotional harmony, physical pleasure, and spiritual understanding that I'd been seeking without even fully appreciating it myself. We then fully enjoyed a deeply beautiful, monogamous, tantric vibrational relationship until she passed away peacefully in my arms in February 2022. Our love was unconditional; we were free spirits choosing to be as one, choosing to stay together and live in blissful harmony. We were not needy of each other or had any expectation of each other. We were joined in sacred union. Anything that affected the other emotionally was discussed openly, rather than being communicated in hurtful ways as can be commonly seen.

Once we had committed to share each other's lives, we also decided to devote our time to helping others achieve the same

Chapter 1: Lionel's Perspective: *Introducing Heart Freedom*

joy and understanding that has given us so much pleasure and so many blessings in life. Perhaps some background to my life may put more perspective into the fold. I never knew what freedom really felt like until I re-found love. The unconditional love for your children or parents doesn't offer the physical intimacy and emotional building blocks we need to be fulfilled. Love is the connector that allows us to receive all by giving all. Like happiness, the more love we give, the more the Universe gives us back.

What an amazingly blessed life I have led. From fairly meagre beginnings of no more than any other fourth born child to a working-class family, I feel I have received so much that I often well up in appreciation and gratitude. I don't even feel as though I deserve the blessings of love and health and wealth and family connection, and all the things that are around me that make life so wonderful. And yet I am blessed beyond my ability, beyond my intelligence, and even beyond the wildest dreams I had as a young man. Now though, I can dream much bigger, much clearer, and much easier, I can only put this down to the freedom to be the me that I was born to be, or Heart Freedom as we've come to call it in our classes.

To be free in our heart we need to be free in our life. To find the relationships that create and elevate us to spiritual joy, to feel the expansion of our being through physical flow, and to be clear of blockages so we can be our true self without any emotional turmoil.

In reality, none of these things are easy to achieve individually. Collectively the order becomes even taller, but please don't for one moment think it's impossible or even difficult. Why can't it happen for you if it can happen for me?

I'd like to give you an overall view of my life so far, of the things that deeply hurt and affected me and the seemingly simple things that happened to rectify the pattern that is still a part of my overall story.

We all have patterns in our life that repeat, we commonly make the same mistakes over and over again. Perhaps some spring to your mind right now or maybe they are more subtle for you.

My Mum and Me

Socrates is acclaimed to have worded, 'Above all else know thyself.' How well do you know the things that have affected your emotional, physical, and spiritual self? I hope my journey thus far will help you find a better route to a rosy future so that your conscious awareness, and that of all other humans, is elevated by the energy you put out into the ether.

There's always been a lion in me

A cycle that shaped my life

The youngest of four siblings, or any number, is probably the easiest place to be raised. Some may not agree. Whilst you may have the other children's cast offs, leftovers, or even receive the rough end of their own problems, in general I would say that older children take the pressure off the youngest. That isn't necessarily a good thing and numerous cases of controlling youngest siblings, have certainly come to my attention over recent years.

It wasn't uncommon in the early sixties to be raised with some religious fervour. The whole church thing was, and still is to my mind, intended to exercise a medium of control on people of all ages. What sort of image is a bleeding dying man in a loincloth nailed to a cross supposed to portray to a young child? It certainly isn't something you'd want to emanate, so it 'makes' you be good according to the ten commandments. Of course, if we were all just to follow those simple rules, the world would be a much better place now. We started church as soon as we could walk in our family. Perhaps having my eldest sister as my Sunday School teacher lulled me into a false sense of security.

When I was a tender innocent of just four years old, my first real run in with a female teacher scarred me for life. Being accused of lying over money I was admonished with humiliation in front of my whole class and left in tears. She abused my faith in women, authority, wealth, and respect for anything good. It took over forty years to properly remember the incident let alone try to heal the harm she had done. The whole occurrence may not have lasted longer than a few minutes, but its emotional damage affected me in ways that I can only surmise. I can now put the experience down to learning, but what if I hadn't had the healing in my late forties? I could still be struggling with not understanding why things didn't flow as I now know they could have done and do now.

Cycles repeat themselves and at a still gentle age of 11 years old I was again wrongly accused by a female headmistress, this time of lying, playing truant, and avoiding the wrath of authority. When you are naïve, and you are brutally told what you are perceived to be; that is the most likely thing you will become. I certainly made sure, from that day on, that wagging school was a priority of life. With seasoned aplomb I soon became a crafty dodger of anything relating to learning. Spending time anywhere but in the classroom became an ambition if not an obsession. Of course, when a young lad is not under the control of those entrusted with his welfare, he then becomes open to the vagaries of others whose own lives

Chapter 1: Lionel's Perspective: *Introducing Heart Freedom*

had suffered similarly or potentially even worse injustices. It gave me the excuse I didn't need to turn my back on the Church of England too.

Money always seemed to be in short supply in the early seventies, even though most people were happier with what they didn't have. That made jumble sales popular. For those who don't know, a jumble sale was an afternoon or evening of chaotic scrambling, mad clambering, and ferocious elbows to get second-hand items, mainly of unironed clothes, from piles of unwanted, often unfashionable donations at prices that were fair and negotiable. People were somehow more able to put their own slant on the way they looked in those days. The modern equivalent has seen charity shops and car boot sales become a similar, perhaps a less tumultuously favoured activity.

It was just one such scramble for a look to impress the ladies, whose attributes were coming to my eager teenage attention, that resulted in what can only be described as the saving of a young soul.

My Grandad died right at the beginning of the seventies. Eight people lived in our house in those days. He wasn't sleeping in our lounge long before he lay there with pre-decimal pennies weighing down his eyelids. As my father worked hard, my Grandad was the man I felt most connected to and protected by as a small child. In the full flow of jumble sale hysteria, instead of some funky tank top or disco dangerous duds catching my eye, a book falls into my hands that brings a shaft of light like a message from heaven beaming into my crazy new teenage mixed-up life. I noticed the photo of an old man on the cover. It reminded me of my Grandad. Turning it over I couldn't even pronounce the author's name. 'Think on These Things' was a curious title though. I opened a page at random, 'intelligence is not knowledge' - the words shone out as if highlighted. I turned to another page, 'most young people don't feel secure because they are frightened' - again the sentence jumped out at me. Another page said, 'the man who says he knows is already dead'. For a princely sum of two new pence, I acquired the book that somehow led me back to the straight and narrow.

It wasn't that book itself, or any other book by Jiddu Krishnamurti, the Indian philosopher, that took me down a path of spiritual awakening, but that book certainly pointed me in the right direction. It got me to change my outlook and my understanding, such that I was open and willing to seek out more value from myself so I could give more value of myself.

The cycles of my life haven't stopped, they are beyond my control. As recently as three years ago, two 'spiritual' women teachers whose ego and bigotry were a closed book, accused, abused and again admonished me. Leaving me feeling very alone and humiliated, they showed no compassion, no empathy, and no forgiveness, they were certainly not capable of understanding the love that they portrayed to render. It's not the things that happen to us that make us who we are, but the way we deal with them. We can hold onto emotions, bottle them up within us and then see them later in obesity, physical illness, or mental problems possibly years down the line.

Learning to clear our conscious and our subconscious minds and to refill them with positive actions should be a daily practice. The more we do, the brighter we are in every respect. It's not so much about breaking the cycles, they are possibly predetermined for our guidance, it's about learning from those cycles and using the messages to direct us down the path of least resistance. Within the practice I now teach are various visualizations. One gives a choice of three routes.

Chapter 1: Lionel's Perspective: *Introducing Heart Freedom*

The orange route is to go back down the road we've already travelled to be able to reassess and hopefully not make similar mistakes again. The white path is the obvious route to take us to wherever we want to go and to have whatever we want. The black road is to take our light and shine it for others to see and gain from our experience, to step into our fears and face the demons.

From my early working life and through my various businesses, I gained the blessings of material wealth, however, nothing has brought me more joy, than being able to work with and help other people's relationships. It was a revelation for me that the material success that had been afforded to me, was not down to what I did so much, as it was to the relationships I had with people, and how easily I could connect with those whom I really valued.

I fell into relationship guidance when people I knew passed on my details to others who were having difficulties. For some reason they thought I would be able to help. I'm so glad they did and still do, there is an amazing comfort in the value others put in my ability, far beyond anything I would want to charge for my services. You don't have to be in a difficult relationship to gain from my work either. Even if you're single, have never had a proper loving relationship in your life, or have a satisfying partnership, my conscious connection work known as Seven Jewels is designed to give anyone and everyone a new perspective on their relationship with themselves, with their partners or family, and their relationship with spirit.

Many people don't realize that they need more than a physical connection, more than an emotional connection and even more than a spiritual connection to find a truly loving relationship – they need them all. The balance that comes from being able to connect on all levels is the real value of finding your own Heart Freedom.

BELIEVE IN LOVE

Chapter 2
Seven Steps to Success

The following exercise is one of the first we offer in our Wellness Workshops.

This part of the book is particularly useful if you have any confusion over your intentions for the future or are in any doubt as to why you do what you do, and what you could potentially be doing to make you happier from now on.

The seven following questions might not be instantly answerable dependent on your current position in life. You may have to consider how you can modify individual questions to fit with your situation or understanding. Take the time to think through them all individually and answer them to your best ability before moving on. A guide to finding your Heart Freedom starts with taking a step back to enable you to see your present position, your ultimate purpose, and the pathway to getting there.

1. What have been the biggest moments of joy and fulfilment in your life to date?

2. What have been the greatest sources of contentment from your chosen career or the work you currently do?

3. What do you absolutely love to do in your personal life?

4. What are your own best natural abilities and talents?

5. What single thing would you most like to see accomplished in the world as it is today?

6. What is the most important thing you would like to achieve in your own life?

7. What are the relationships between, or the common denominators of your answers?

Chapter 2: Seven Steps to Success

Once you have answered the seven questions above, you can begin to formulate how your answers fit into the three elements of existence. Everything and everyone exists in a trilogy of its/their physical presence, its/their emotional energy and its/their spiritual synergy. These can be seen as equal amounts that make up the whole of anything.

For us to fully understand ourselves and our ability, the flow of energy we put out into the world, we need to realize the effects the trilogy is having on our daily life, and how that can make a difference to others and ultimately ourselves.

Knowing your own personal values will give you the physical presence of how you show up in the world, and how others see you or want to be connected to you in a physical sense. How they want to work with you, think of you or just be around you.

Finding your purpose in life is the most directed thing you can accomplish, it will guide you to freedom through clearing emotional blockages so that your natural instinctive, intuitive, innocence can flow through. This is what other people adhere to. It's not just the way you look that makes you attractive, it's not just what you say that makes others want to connect with you, it's the energy you give off as a whole package, physically, emotionally, and spiritually.

Faith creates a complete trust or confidence in certain outcomes that need no proof or confirmation other than your conviction to believe. Once you have a belief in your ultimate destiny you do not need to question your motives or the reality of any outcome, it is what it is. That sense of deep knowing, is the connector between the elements that produces integrity. This provides joy and happiness on a scale that is then only determined by external factors out of your control.

Being intrinsically happy is the essential and natural way to live with passion, in peace, with positivity and in the power of love. It's the road to enlightenment.

Once we have the basic concerns out of the way like; how we need to make an income, what level of wealth satisfies us, where we want to live etc. our time becomes more a tool to create value for others. By using this guide to find the physical success we desire, we can move forward to understand more about ourselves and how we can find our own Heart Freedom.

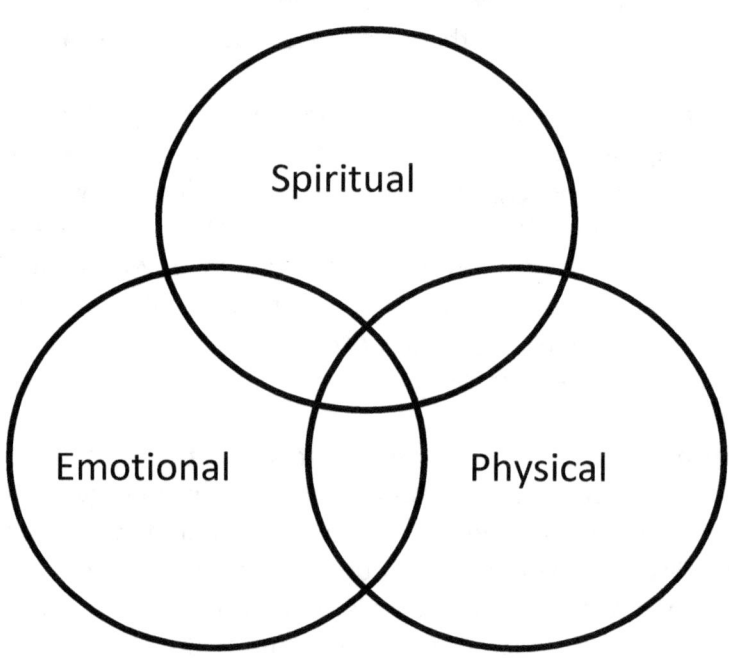

Chapter 3
Intentions and Objectives

Finding your own Heart Freedom can only exist with intention. Intention creates objectives. Your objectives can relate to different energy zones within the body. These are commonly known as chakras of which there is an enormous amount of often conflicting information already available and accessible to all. We won't go into the details of direct usage or the power of the chakras here, other than to say they should not be taken irreverently and that more depth of knowledge in this area can be found through our classes and events.

The objective of each intention can come from the purpose of each chakra and its position within the body. These should all flow with passion, peace and positivity found in the presence of love.

The Crown Chakra works with the conscious mind, with faith, healing and understanding. The objective works around having the knowledge of what you want and why.

The Third Eye Chakra works with the subconscious mind, visualization, clarity of thought, and being able to see the bigger picture in detail. The objective works around seeing the present position, the direction or pathway in life and the ultimate purpose or destination.

The Throat Chakra works with communication, what we see and our perspective, what we hear and how we emote our feelings, and what we say to others and how that is accepted by them. The objective is the power to create, to get things done and to be humble in the process.

The Heart Chakra works with love, with compassion, empathy, and forgiveness. The objective is the connection with others, no expectation of others, becoming more whole and being respected and trusted for what you are.

The Solar Plexus Chakra works with energy to clear blockages, create good health and be spiritually connected. The objective is to find emotional freedom, be physically able to create your ultimate purpose and to be joyfully happy.

The Sacral Chakra works with awareness, acceptance, and appreciation. The objective is in valuing what is real and important, understanding how things coexist and appreciating the source and spirit of everything.

The Base Chakra works with praise, respect, and thankfulness. The objective is to connect and give gratitude for the past, the present and the future of all that is, all that we are and all that will ever be.

By examining your world in this way, particularly if you can do it on a daily basis, you can create a clear mission for your life that will sustain your personal responsibility to be aware of and accept or change the patterns of the way you think, feel and act. This in turn will create actions from your decision-making process based on your ultimate purpose. Your whole energy then becomes based and directed on your intentions and objectives, rather than on the malaise of energies (many negative) that attach to each of us, every minute of every day, through the varying forces and variable frequencies of the energies of everything that surrounds us all.

All self-inquiries tend to lead on to bigger questions, some of which we hope to answer in our next book. You may prefer to join one of our classes, events, retreats, workshops, or free circles, where we would love to welcome you to one of our highly regarded retreats around the globe.

Please email your questions to lionel@lionelpalatine.com

Chapter 4
Finding Love

Limbic resonance is a term for a mechanism that connects mother and child through the emotional centres of their brains. Sharing biological rhythms enables a sensing of each other's feelings and can be developed when we are open to another's energy.

First attractions are often physical in nature but for a deeper relationship there really needs to be an emotional bond that can allow communications on a much more connected level. When in balance, the physical, the emotional, and the spiritual elements of a resonance combine to make an unstoppable force. How do we know when we have a connection that will mature into a good relationship? Is it just physical lust, or is it something far more powerful? How can we assess the value of our feelings for another? What is the difference between love and lust and just what are the essential ingredients of physical lust, love, or a spiritual connection?

Lust is the simple physical passion; love like all things on any plane is an energy but finding your Heart Freedom is something more than both combined, it is another level of connection, a deeper value that sets both people free. Love is far more than just a simple direct energy though, with passion added it's extra powerful. The essence of love is brought about by the harmony of three essential elements which connect the previously mentioned seven chakra points within the bodies of the sender and receiver of an energy. Love's energy can be felt through any or all the chakra points collectively.

Passion or lust is more likely to be felt through individual chakras. Any one chakra can connect with the same chakra in another person, or with all the chakras of another person creating a divine matrix or a seemingly endless combination of personality traits and potential feelings. Each chakra has three harmonic elements, each of which can connect to the same elements within any of the seven chakras in another person.

By investigating our own elementary make up, we can analyze our energy for love and be able to establish exactly what we need from another person. We should be able to determine our desires and needs to mirror our own personality. The path of true love may never be easy but by knowing our own personality, we can begin to appreciate what we are looking for in another before we begin to seek out that person. Most things in life can be left to chance but you can certainly narrow down the possibility of finding your own sex God/Goddess by following simple rules.

You can grasp the personal depth of clarity and connection with the Divine Source of Consciousness (God, or your own interpretation) which ultimately determines your life. A good starting point maybe to look at your highest values, to determine where those values fit within you and prioritize your thinking. You've hopefully already found some answers in the Seven Steps exercise earlier. Later we'll see how each of your elements fit within the trilogy of Emotional, Physical and Spiritual connection. Suffice to say for now that your highest three values should be enough to learn the lessons of pleasure over pain.

For me now it's easy and unquestionable: health, love and growth cover most of my life's wants, needs and desires. Select your own interpretation of your greatest gifts and transfix them into your thinking. Without our health, most of which is connected to our emotions, we struggle to move forward in any respect. Whether you already have love, seek love, or want to expand love, its strengths can never really be underestimated, and its power can change anything and everything. True security in life comes from knowing that every

Chapter 4: Finding Love

day we are in some way improving it, our quality of life becomes of little concern when each day is getting better than the one before. Any small improvement advances where we were, to where we are right now. Living in the now is the key to creating happiness of where we want to be.

Completing the exercises within this book will help enable you to find the love of your dreams. Begin today to build the vision of love in your mind's eye.

BELIEVE IN LOVE

Chapter 5
The Fear of Loss

Subconsciously we covet everything that makes us happy.

There is a mental fear of loss within you which is your own personal barrier to having everything you want, including the love you desire. The negative thinking that you may lose love, stops you from receiving love in its full empowerment because you restrict giving it unconditionally. Emotional negativity can be transferred from parent to child from conception onwards. You may not even know you have it or why. Any loss that a mother grieves over, could be transferred into a subconscious emotional trait of her children, particularly a child in the womb through limbic resonance.

When we suffer loss, especially if it's one of our protectors, like a parent or one that we protect like a child, that loss is instinctively embedded in our internal makeup, and potentially seriously imbalances our emotional, physical, and spiritual elements. Each of us passes any loss of our auric energy onto our offspring, and also onto anyone else that comes into our aura. Only when we meet a soul mate with the harmonizing factors to our own trilogy could we possibly have the balance to create pure love through passion, peace and positivity that would bring about Heart Freedom.

Your own lack of willingness to give love away will create the fear of loss and lack of love. This simple fear of loss can show itself in everything we say, do and feel. Once you are awakened to the facts, you can think about how you can change your own beliefs and patterns to bring about your biggest desires. By focusing on the fear of loss that's exactly what you'll bring about: more loss.

What you think about you bring about.

BELIEVE IN LOVE

Even if you fear loss in something like your finances, you can bring it about in another area like your love life. Knowing exactly what you want is important, so you know just where to focus your thinking.

Think about your fears and write down here what may be holding you back:

Chapter 6
Barriers

Anger, fear, and greed are seen in some religions as curses that prevent people from entering the Kingdom of Heaven. I believe we can create our own Heaven right here on Earth. Instead of curses, I like to look at them as barriers to keep us all going in the right direction. Without having some part of these barriers, you are likely to be destitute or living a reckless life. However, by releasing inhibitions you remove the barriers and can attract your desires with ease.

Like the limbic resonance between mother and child, you can create a sort of magnetic resonance that can bring you everything you want as soon as you stop wanting it. It's all down to appreciation and gratitude really. Your self-worth is far more valuable than your love is worth to another person, but your relationship to love must be motivated by purpose and joy. Specific incidents can easily affect your thinking and thereby your emotional state. Without the right mindset for love you're not going to be able to attract it. Worse still, some people by thinking wrongly, could attract everything they don't want instead of any of the things they do. Your beliefs and understandings are based on your interpretations of your experiences. These may not necessarily be the actual experience at all, they are just your interpretations.

So, you must never have your motivation for love based in anger, fear, or greed. To break down the barriers to love you must wholeheartedly believe that you are supposed to be loved and must love yourself fully. Using the different chakra points as references, you can begin to see love as a match to your own ability, to do all the things you do. Combine this with the emotional ability to feel and communicate clearly and a love connection becomes more likely. It only then requires a spiritual ability to understand certain things such as belief, vision, and gratitude to complete the trilogy that creates love, provided you can leave your ego behind of course.

Think of your barriers and write down here what needs to be overcome:

Chapter 7
Motivation

The lack of love is not a problem but a symptom of a problem.

To permanently change your ability to love and your acceptance of love you must first change your inner world. The process to motivate love must start with the inner game. What thoughts, feelings, actions, and results are happening in your life right now? You must be aware of where you are in the present to be able to move forward. Your beliefs are only what you hold to be true, they may not actually be true even though they taint your view of everything.

Your thinking creates your actions and it's those actions which create your results. There is no negative to love, only the meaning you give it. Whatever you believe will be, will be. So, if you believe you do not have enough love in your life, you will not have enough love in your life. When you believe you always attract the wrong sort of person, that's exactly who you will attract. What is your current situation around love? Are you unsure of your beliefs? Just look at the results so far, are they what you asked for? When you know what your beliefs actually are, and how they can be restricting you, you can look at ways to change those beliefs. When you realize that the conclusions you have come to are only your illusions, you can reverse the thinking to bring about what you really want.

Choose to love and be loved and you will be.

When you give out love to everyone, every day, that same love will come back to you many times over. Try to examine what has happened in your life to create the beliefs you now hold around relationships. What specific incidents have led to your way of thinking? Determine to change negative thinking; do not presume your thoughts to be right. Understanding your own mind, body and spirit is essential to knowing you have the ability to achieve your dreams.

You can either choose to be right or you can choose to be happy.

What thinking do you hold to be true that could be negatively affecting you right now?

Chapter 8
Mind of Love

What beliefs do you hold to be true that could be affecting you right now? Are there any links to your thinking that bring about happy relationship memories? A song perhaps, a place or maybe an object. You need to be able to interrupt any negative thinking around love and turn it into a positive thought. By using an image or song that can break the pattern of negative love thoughts, you can bring about positive relationship thoughts. Your inner world and imagination will create your outer world reality. There is no point thinking you will enjoy love when it arrives. If you are not ready for it, you might not even see it or be able to manage it when it comes along.

Learn to give love and you will be ready to receive love.

Create a habit of thinking loving thoughts, seeing the best in everyone you know, everyone you meet and everyone you think about. Then just see how enjoyable your life becomes as you become more attractive by what you give out. Pay attention to your thoughts, whenever a negative thought comes to mind around any relationship; replace it with a song or image that brings happy memories. Make it a habit to change your thinking to find your own Heart Freedom. Whatever has gone before, put it behind you, don't dwell on it or it will shackle you for life. Put yourself first, don't get hung up on other people's opinions or judgements of you. Set your own morals and values to live by.

Where your attention goes, energy flows and the result shows.

The way you interpret other people's thoughts of you may be completely wrong, and even if not, it simply doesn't matter.

BELIEVE IN LOVE

Your love is between your head and heart and that of the person you love or will love – no one else. Begin to realize the potential you hold within yourself to create whatever you want and leave others out of it.

Make a list here of all the positive love memories you can remember:

Chapter 9
One True Love

Just like religion, I couldn't advocate that there can be only one true belief of love. This is a rapidly advancing world, we should all be growing, learning, understanding, and changing to cope with it.

Loving today may not be the same as loving tomorrow.

When we love it can be wholeheartedly, but it can also be one sided. Any and every relationship can and generally does ebb and flow.

We must see that there can be an imbalance in any relationship, due to the effects of life happening around all of us all the time. When one part of the trilogy of a connection is out of kilter with the partners energies, the relationship can become strained. This can be difficult to enjoy or even manage sometimes. The differences in the particular energies can be balanced across the elements, but unless they begin to equalize there is little hope long term. Any imbalance across the elements can neutralize, providing it is equaled overall. For example, one partner could easily have greater physical energy counterbalanced by the other partner's greater spiritual energy.

With a new relationship you may not be able to find any faults with your partner. You have to be careful you are not just infatuated as in time to come; the slightest annoyance could present a big problem.

You don't need to look for faults in the other person, but you do need to recognize that none of us are perfect and accept each other as we are. When something about someone else annoys you, ask yourself what that is showing in you and why that is a problem for you. It may reveal some interesting failings in your own character.

The primary reason for us to love is to be loved.

Make a list of ideal personality traits you want in a partner:

Chapter 10
To Love or Not to Love

We all need some degree of love. Like with most things, the more of it we practice, the more of it we will attract and receive. We must realize that everyone has the potential to connect with the Divine Source of Consciousness and through that connection can manifest their heart's desires.

Above all else you need to know yourself, so you can focus your imagination on what you truly want or against what you don't want.

Focus creates reality and tension seeks swift resolution.

Your health, your financial wealth, your love-life, or lack of it, is all based on what you have or have not been doing. Everything you have ever said and done, every decision you have ever made, and everything you have ever thought before now, has brought you to where you are right now. It's never too late to have the relationship you want, provided you can first focus on the relationship with yourself.

Meeting the right person in the right place at the right time is only possible if you have the right attitude, to see it, realize it, and grasp it with both hands before it's gone. The key to finding true love is to raise your energy levels to attract it and then seize it when it comes.

Everything is a result of cause and effect.

Celebrate other people's love, don't be jealous of it. Learn about love and invest in yourself to be more attractive for yourself and to love yourself more (not for sex). Determine what the message you give out is saying about you. Who are you attracting by the way you look? What energy are you giving off and how are you being seen?

A good lover should be clean (of mind and body), full of fun, able to communicate easily, not needy or have any expectations.

To give out good energy, you must have the right belief in yourself. You should never be held back by your negative thinking. Your own self beliefs can generally be based on misconceptions, as you perceive most things differently to the way others see those same things in you.

An emotional blockage from your childhood could hold you back for your entire life, and yet the person who created that blockage may well have an entirely different viewpoint of the incident or may not even hold any conscious memory of it. To them, it could have just been completely insignificant. Much of what you believe about yourself is formed by habitual thinking, giving wrong answers to your doubts.

To manifest what you want, you need to work on your own thoughts and feelings to create your actions and results.

What is your personal love message saying about you and how can it be improved?

Chapter 11
Beliefs

How do you feel, think, and act around love? Be aware of where you are right now! Beliefs are what you hold to be true. Your beliefs colour your views of love. Your beliefs are not based on actual experiences but on your interpretation of those experiences.

Nothing has meaning other than the meaning you give it.

Don't necessarily believe anything you say or think to yourself. Learn to detach yourself from your thoughts through meditation. When a negative thought comes into your head; just say to yourself "thank you for sharing that thought." Decide if any thought supports your ambition to be loved and if not, replace it with more supporting thoughts. Do not take anything you hear personally.

Remove negative thoughts, words, beliefs, and images from your life. Learn to spread your love and trust other people. Update your beliefs around love on a regular basis. Create a personal supporting belief around the positive aspects of love. Feel the energy of love.

Change and update your own personal love thoughts as you go along. Build a sentence or sing a line that epitomizes your love thoughts to bring the right perspective to your emotions. Try to use a love mantra that is short, positive and in the present tense. Make it slow and emotional. Use it every day at the same time to bring about the relationship experience you want. Nobody is stopping you from achieving your true love experiences other than you.

Treat everything as a game, you are everything in the game of love. Create your own vision of what love means to you. Let your mind picture, hear, and feel the partner and relationship you want. Bring it into your life everyday by using any quiet time to make your visualizations more real, more colourful, more dynamic. Add to the same picture each time you close your eyes, so you have perfect clarity on who and what you want to create in your life. Never put a limit on what you can achieve, build from your mind not fanaticism.

What are your beliefs around love? List them here:

Chapter 12
Are You Worthy of Love?

Poor receivers of love generally feel unworthy of being loved. Their looks, shape, fears, intelligence etc. conditions them into thinking they have no right to be loved.

You are worthy of love simply because you exist.

You are equal to and as deserving of love as the next person. We are all equal in the divine matrix of life. Each of us consists of energy, how that energy resonates is the only difference between anyone and anything. For everyone who gives, there must be a receiver, each are needed by the other and exist in duality. It is far better to be in a position to be able give love, than the desperately needy and vulnerable position of wanting to receive it without question.

The Universe has an abundant supply of love, if you think yourself unworthy, you will not be ready to receive it and your share will go elsewhere. In giving unconditionally you can also learn to receive in the same way. So, when you start to receive compliments and good feelings from others, you need to be able to accept those feelings generously and gratefully without the need to return anything.

Whether you are worthy or not is just your story. It doesn't mean anything, it's not real. Again, nothing has meaning except the meaning you give it. Say to yourself that you are worthy of love, and you are, if you say that you are unworthy of love in any way, that's exactly what you'll be. So, who is going to make you worthy other than you? Change your own story so it empowers you to give love and be loved. Practice receiving love in your visualizations, raise your energy and start attracting that love into your life.

When you receive a compliment or an indication that your own thinking is improving, openly declare it to yourself and give thanks. Do not judge whatever comes your way, just be grateful and practice the emotion of gratitude over any previous feelings of unworthiness. How special are you just to have been born? Value it.

Rewrite any story about relationships that is not serving your higher good:

Chapter 13
Seek Love

Seek Love and ye shall find Love! Energy attracts. When you're in the right place emotionally, physically, and spiritually, at the right time, you'll get all the love and passion you deserve from what you attract.

The way you do anything is the way you do everything.

By changing your approach to love even slightly, you may get a very different result. To become successful in love we must let go of our old angers, resentment, and hang-ups. We all do the best we can with the knowledge we have. Forgive those who have wronged you and let your stress and anger go. They are holding you back; it's all about you now, not them. Anyone who is stopping you from moving forward on your path to happiness needs to be ridden from your life. Use visualizations to complete whatever unfinished business there is to your satisfaction. Write them a letter putting the grievance right, and then ceremoniously burn it, tear it up or throw it in a river. Set yourself up for success not failure; do not expect anything in return from them. Do not hold onto incomplete communications. Have the capacity to forgive; life is just too short for holding onto grievances, it just brings you more pain in the end. We can suggest other techniques if you prefer.

Don't be too hard on yourself either. Recognize and acknowledge your successes. Success in love will bring more success. Look around you and see other people in love, and realize if they can love, so can you. Look at what's right, not what's wrong. Pat yourself on the back for every success no matter how small. Build an inner confidence by forcing yourself to focus on your successes. Try writing a daily journal of your loving thoughts and actions. Celebrate any action that pushes you forwards. Nurture your spirit and your inner child. Through the instinctive intuition of your innocence, you will find the love you desire most. Create positive references to endorse your confidence to feel and find love for yourself.

Visualize and write here all you can about the person you want to love:

Chapter 14
Your Own Love Beliefs

One of the most prevalent beliefs stopping people from receiving love is the need for self-reverential love and approval; the thinking that you are either unworthy of love or unlovable. This can often be a type of depression or signs of depressive tendencies. Some people seek love only to reject it when offered. There can be a thinking to put others first and thereby deny your own need by having to help anyone but yourself. To prove your belief that there is nothing worth loving about you, you subconsciously set yourself up for rejection. Once you have attracted and taken the steps to belong, you will do the opposite to prove your inner self belief to be right. This can make you the centre of controversy or make you overdramatic to test whether people will still accept you and still love you. You may set too high standards and continuously punish yourself. By taking everything personally, the belief can become questioning of everything you have. A type of paranoia creeps in where you become completely over sensitive to others' opinions. This brings about a necessity to break off relationships before the other person discovers how unworthy you think you are.

Does this sound like you? Perhaps it's time to dismiss self-questioning like "what does that say about me?" Or "how does that relate to me?" Replace them with an attitude of self-belief and focus on the beauty of nature. Let your thoughts become part of a larger picture where you're one of many, perhaps a blade of grass or a tree in the forest. See your questions as weeds to be plucked from a beautiful garden so you are left with only good thoughts about yourself. Get out into a forest and feel the positivity of trees, let them breathe in your self-doubts as you experience nature, naturally and peacefully. Make a list of all the things that make you worthy of being

BELIEVE IN LOVE

loved and place it in a prominent place like the bathroom, so you'll see it every day. Read it out aloud or chant it into a mirror as often as you can to affirm your self-worth.

Make a list here of all the things that make you worthy of love:

Chapter 15
Learning to Love

We all have a need to be constantly growing either by learning or progressing towards a chosen goal or ultimate purpose. Love is no different in so much as we need to be continuously learning to love more, or be loved more, or preferably both. You should be guided by those who are already in love, see how they choose their feelings with each other and the world around them. Try to enjoy their feelings and understand their thinking so you know what you're aiming for. Always finish what you start, build the mindset to learn more about yourself and build the picture of the lover you seek. Create the intention by visualizing the looks, the personality even the career of the person you want in your life. Make a vision board that represents all the attributes your new partner will have and then write a statement from your heart of your specification. Put this letter out to the Universe to manifest into your life exactly what you want, then put it out of your mind, don't dwell on the fact you haven't got it yet. Create the vision, build on it and make it a part of your life's daily rituals, but don't be attached to it either. You have to be able to be able to let go of the very things you want most for them to come into your life.

Be intentional that your purpose for love is your life mission.

To be truly happy we need to live in the purpose of our life. It is worth being risk averse as it can be all too easy to grasp at things and feel stressed when we are desperate. To create a better world around you, you need to create a better you. Share what you learn, be generous with what you know and your feelings towards others. Make a difference to yourself and every other person by thinking positively about all the people in your life. Look for the good in everyone you meet. You are either affecting everyone and being affected by them or you are infecting them with your spirit of love. Are you raising your game or putting others down?

Start to write here the story of how the future of your life will look:

Chapter 16
Clear Yourself for Love

Your old experiences, beliefs, and ways of acting with relationships need regular examination and clearing to allow new love into your life. Writing two lists can really help. Write one list of negative relationship experiences and the other of positive events. The positive list can be added to your vision board to help create the same types of happenings in your new relationship.

The negative list could be depressive, but it can also give you an idea of what to avoid. Furthermore, you can use this list to establish any unfinished business which needs clearing from your head and life. There may be lingering feelings from past relationships that are blocking your way forward. There may be situations where communications have not been good, leaving things unsaid. There could be doubts or long-term feelings of resentment or anger about things that were done or said to you or by you. By listing all the relationship blockages, you become aware of the problems you need to tackle. By bearing grudges or being preoccupied by the past, you hurt only yourself, you need to be able to project forgiveness to open the potential possibilities available to you.

Forgiveness frees the forgiver and even if it is a challenge, repeatedly coming back to it will eventually allow you the freedom to move on. Forgiving is not about condoning someone else's behaviour, it's about accepting what has happened, releasing any anger or resentment, and allowing yourself to be free from old relationships to enable you to empower yourself to let new relationships in. Whenever negative thoughts around previous relationships come into your head, you need to park them out of the way to give yourself the mentality for love.

Ceremoniously destroy the negative list for maximum value and effect. Keep the positive list for future reference.

What are your love requirements to make you happy? List them here:

Chapter 17
Let Love Flow

When you put labels on things you stop yourself from doing things that could come naturally if just allowed to flow. Do not let labels spoil your game of love, enjoy the search, make it fun and don't have regrets. Be proactive and be positively in charge of what you want to achieve. Get out of your comfort zone, act in spite of fear, act in spite of doubt, act in spite of worry over the repercussions. Only your actions will dispel your fears, procrastination just causes regrets as opportunities pass you by. Question how many problems you have around relationships that are not real, they're just in your head. Hesitation causes pain, when your eyes meet another's don't shy away, look deep and take action that will help you gain love. Don't be afraid of asking for help from those who obviously have loving relationships. Find out how and where their love was born but remember to be natural. Even vulnerability can be attractive in a safe place and can lead to so much more. Knowledge of exactly what you want, solid written intentions of your heart's desires, will help you overcome fear. Be courageous, you are not your mind, what your head tells you is only your perception of anything. You don't have to be needy; you don't have to be lacking, and you don't have to accept anybody else's negative attitude or opinion.

You don't need anyone's approval to live the way you want.

Live from your purpose and for the joy of life. Don't stick with some job you hate just to pay the bills. We all need to earn a living, but we can survive and often be happier on much less. Look at relationships from a place of strength not weakness, be courageous not fearful. Honour your truth and if you like the energy of someone don't be afraid of letting them know.

BELIEVE IN LOVE

Think in terms of your word being law. Approve of yourself, you don't need anyone else's vote of favour to do what you want. Train yourself to overcome your fears and build your confidence to succeed. Follow your heart in every way you can.

Working from your intuitive, innocence, what are your love needs?

Chapter 18
What Sort of Love do You Want?

More freedom to follow your heart's passion is worth far more than the ability to pay for things you don't really need. When you have set your goals, go for them wholeheartedly. Consider what you are going to change about yourself that will help the way your energy is seen by others. Ask yourself what type of person are you looking for? Many people tend to put everyone into stereotypical boxes. This may make life and contacts more manageable but, when it comes to love, you could easily overlook the very things or person that could bring you true happiness. When you make a decision based on some group or type of person that you think will not suit you, you're potentially missing an opportunity to meet a whole host of people.

Everyone knows someone... think about the way you categorize people and whether that is serving your best interests and potential for relationships. When you put people into stereotypes you create a subconscious expectation of them, and by the incredible law of attraction, that is often just what you'll bring about, the very type of person you don't want. You really must listen to what you are saying to yourself. Think about your own thoughts and write them down so you review, assess, and change your own thinking. Listen to what you say to others too and ask them how they feel about certain people in your life. Their answers may give you some insight into how your beliefs are attracting those people into your life, or not attracting what you really want in a relationship. Bringing your attention to the rights or wrongs of who you are presently attracting, gives you the opportunity to sort out your thinking so you can attract the very personality you desire most.

BELIEVE IN LOVE

Once you know exactly what you want or don't want, throw out any thinking that doesn't serve the final goal. See your thinking as something you can throw away and when you've made that visible image see yourself putting it out with the kitchen rubbish.

Write out your love vision here, your story of real joy as you want it to be:

Chapter 19
Your Love Type

When you have cleared the space in your head to allow in the desires of your heart, you can begin to think about what kind of people you are currently attracting into your life and why. We all have different wants, needs and desires. Once you have achieved the basic needs of life's comforts and security, you can look to increase what you give and receive.

When you know what you want to receive from a partner, you can communicate those wishes to receive your wants. Likewise, when you know what your partner wants to receive, you can give those desires to enhance the loving relationship. Knowing what type of love you want, can lead you to your love partner. Knowing what type of love they want, can enable you to satisfy their every desire.

Giving and receiving the satisfaction of another's desires can create the balance that can enhance real love. Find any relationship that works well and there will always be a strong element of giving and receiving. You need to be aware of your own love type if you want to avoid making mistakes that you have previously repeated. To achieve this, you need to observe your current thoughts, preferably with an existing relationship, to know exactly what you want.

Unless you change the thinking about the relationship you want, you run the danger of assigning your mind to the negative thinking that there is no one available to suit you. There is a saying that your thoughts become your words, your words become your actions, your actions become your habits, your habits become your character and your character becomes your destiny.

To change your destiny, you need to change your thinking.

When you can always feel good about yourself, you will always look good in the eyes of others. Listen to yourself and realize the typical things you say to yourself that are negative and rewrite them into positive affirmations.

Every time you realize you are saying something negative about yourself, stop, then talk to your alter ego self. Park the thought, say to your alter ego "thank you for sharing that thought with me." Then replace the thought with a positive thought from your bank of positive affirmations (the same one that's by the bathroom mirror perhaps), good love memories or good feelings. Look at your positive affirmations to decide what type of love you want, and what type of love you can give to another. Write down the typical things you say about yourself and change them into positive thoughts.

Re-write the typical things you say about yourself into positive thoughts:

Chapter 20
Know Thy Own Love

By knowing exactly what you want from your relationship and what you can bring to your partner, you stand a much better chance of creating a more loving, longer lasting, more rewarding, and intimately connected partnership. Over time, your wants, needs and desires all change, yet how much time have you spent uncovering exactly what you want? Asking each other what is important in your relationship not only gives you insight to the other person but also increases communication and bonding. By analyzing what each of you need from the other, over the years ahead, you will be able to focus on each other's objectives to make the relationship more exciting. Whether you are in a relationship or just want to be, periodically reassessing what you want must be a good idea.

When you have a list of wants you can put out your intentions for the Universe to bring you the person who can most fulfil them. So often we can complain about our partner without even knowing about our own wants, let alone communicating those wants to achieve the long-lasting value of the relationship. How can you expect anyone else to know what you want if you don't really know yourself? We can all be too quick to complain when we don't get what we want, but how often do we convey exactly what we do want? You need to ask yourself exactly what is important for you to receive from your relationship.

Again, you could write two lists, one showing what you want from your relationship and the other showing what kind of partner you want. Ask yourself "what is important to me in a partner?" Consider and list all the values you want your partner to have. Try to get a clear picture of your ideal partner and of exactly what you want from that person and from the relationship as a whole. See the vision clearly in your mind's eye on a daily basis and build on it. You'll be surprised how soon it can become a reality.

Write here exactly what you want to receive from a relationship:

Chapter 21
Building Heart Freedom

Let's presume now for a moment that you have found the love of your life, the soul mate with whom you want to share everything. They will only want to share everything with you if they are happy, and totally satisfied with you as their soul mate too.

In young love this can be easy to feel as you tend not to see your own misgivings in them (or what you might consider their faults). They can seemingly do no wrong. They have no annoying habits; they are perfect in every way. A few years down the line however, and the ravages of life, work, families etc. can easily take their toll, and the first person you blame is the person closest to you.

Keeping love a success is very different from finding a lover. There are many things we should do to keep a relationship alive and exciting, but there are three fundamentals to avoid at all costs.

The first of these is competition; a relationship is a union, a harmony, a belief in the other person, not a race of any kind. Each should be glad for the other to do better, achieve or win something as it is a tribute to the relationship, but between the two there should be no winners as each contributes to the other's success and betterment in different ways. Each should be equally responsible for the achievements of the other partner.

Secondly, is complaining about what has been, what is, or what is likely to come. As a unity between partners, either one complaining to the other instead of sharing feelings, will eventually turn the other against them instead of bringing the bond closer together. Communication must take the place of complaint so that each partner is aware of the others' feelings but does not feel criticized or blamed for it.

The third big no-no is compromise; if you are continually giving something up for the other person, resentment won't be far behind. There must always be a willingness to compromise along with the wish to please your partner, but if there are major goals which you want to achieve and you are not supported, the relationship will suffer and eventually fail.

Perhaps you could think of some ways to ensure that you don't cross any fundamentals? You may have more of your own, that you could stipulate within your vision work, and could convey to any prospective partner. A solid connected relationship can build if you consider the three elements of emotional freedom, physical health, and spiritual joy. The most difficult of these to understand may be the spiritual connection. The physical side of a relationship is one thing, but the spiritual connection can enhance the pleasure many fold. It may be too late to create a spiritual bond if you wait until the physical side begins to wane (which it inevitably will). Unfortunately, we seem to have the bigger problem of understanding or accepting the value of a spiritual side to a relationship until much later in life.

Without certainty of a belief there is nothing of value, even if that belief is in nothing (as in no God etc.) at least it is a belief. Whether the understanding behind any belief can be communicated is a separate matter. Our spiritual or believing self, must have an inner knowing that is obvious and potent to us as individuals. No spiritual ritual, thought, or deed has any value without belief, yet we each have our own understanding which should be subject to constant improving or confirmation. Our beliefs do not have to be the same as another person's (even our soul mate's), but for us to be able to enjoy a wonderfully connected and balanced relationship,

Chapter 21: Building Heart Freedom

there must be a basis on which to build a spiritual understanding with the other person.

When you are certain of your own understanding of life (and death), you can rise above your physical and emotional love to a higher love. Finding a partner who is the complementary opposite of your spiritual understanding maybe the most difficult element to fulfil. Once you have discovered physical or sexual reciprocity, and the emotional capacity to stand strong and be supportive of another's emotional needs, the spiritual experience and connection can start to be built. You need clarity, accountability and to be directed by the intuition and integrity from the deepest core of your innocent wisdom. Spiritual direction must be combined with a deep purpose and understanding that a heart of radiance can manifest anything.

To find real spiritual love and Heart Freedom requires a breakthrough into the understanding of, and surrender to, the awareness of oneness, the acceptance of duality, and the appreciation of the trilogy without any form of motivation or ego. The joint spiritual connection can only come about by transcending the fear of loss, surrendering to the spiritual unity of unconditional love, and by going beyond all sense of control as your hearts meet in total abandoned passion, a trance state of pure bliss. Total ravishment and surrender must accompany complete trust in the others heart, with fearlessness to take you to a higher consciousness and to release your bodily world and fulfil your authentic purpose. When you can smile at your negative programming you will rise above your conscious thinking.

There is truth and there is what we each believe to be true. Only responding to the truth and light of your transcendent thoughts will let your attitude develop from what you know to be truth. Therefore, you have to consider what you can do to break down the barriers to a higher spiritual connection in your relationship. The only way to find true Heart Freedom is to find the love you desire through creating the affirmations and visualizations along with clear communication of your desires. Send the messages from your heart but stand strong in your own power to have no attachment to them.

Be appreciative of everything and everyone that comes into your life and give to others with gratitude for your own bodily world. Live with integrity and seek your authentic ultimate purpose. Devote yourself to the love you seek and have gracious feelings of willingness to care for the emotional, physical, and spiritual wellbeing of your lover's soul. Seek the path of ecstasy and give the time to pursue it. Practice as much as possible and learn to climb the ladder of spiritual competence. Ensure you are rooted to the Earth. Realize your true identity and develop your psychic energetic chakra powers, to the point where energy can flow through your individual chakras into your perineum base point (between the genitals and the anus), out to the Earth and in from the Divine Source of Consciousness through your aura to the Earth.

Create the love you want to receive by making the world around you the world you want to experience. Pure love, understanding and consciousness are all forms and realizations of pure energy, above all else know thyself to gain true liberation. Follow your own path and let it attract those who seek you. Live in the joy of others and be gracious in understanding their feelings. Be willing to help and love others without need or expectation of anything in return.

Develop your connections through sharing mental, physical, and spiritual pastimes. Lose your ego and understand we are all equal in birth, in life and in death. Never judge another without assessing yourself first and understand we all exist in oneness and duality at the same time. Search for the attainment of enlightenment as well as spiritual power, and

Chapter 21: Building Heart Freedom

practice self-development with common sense to achieve higher consciousness with greater energy, and ensure you enjoy the process as all that matters.

What are the decisions you have made and need to take immediate action on?

Chapter 22
Creating Heart Freedom

Your daily inspirational practice is the route to creating your emotional, physical, and spiritual freedom. Don't go to the light but let the light be above and behind you to illuminate your path and destination, let your own light shine bright to show the present. Use your own common sense to judge what you accept, believe, and understand. Connect spiritually, but when you are with other 'spiritual' or 'religious' people ask them the golden question to ascertain their understanding: - How do you feel, hear, or see God?

When we lose something of value to us, like our keys, our wallet or heaven forbid our mobile phone, we get agitated, anxious, concerned, or begin to panic. When we lose a piece of our heart, we get emotional pain, loss of connection to ourselves and physical illness can ensue. When our heart gets hurt, for whatever reason, we are emotionally tied and can become devoid of compassion for others and close our hearts. However, when we give the gift of forgiveness, we open our hearts again and can receive bountiful benefits.

Don't just ask to be healthy, also ask to be strong enough to be resilient so you can resist the temptations that can harm you. Open the gates to appreciation so you may fully value everything and be at one with the energies of the Universe and enjoy the awareness of oneness with all thing's animal, mineral and vegetable. Ensure your daily practice gives humble thanks, gives abundant thanks, and gives heartfelt thanks for all that is, all that you are and all that will ever be. Offer your energy back to Mother Earth and the Divine Source of Consciousness, for the life and body you're born into, for the air you breathe, for the water you drink and the food you eat, as well as the beauty you see all around you. Ask for the power of clear perspective of all you see, the correct reception of all you hear and complete acceptance of all you say, so your self-respect is harmonious with all situations you are in. Have clarity of your visualizations and connect with others on a spiritual basis.

Anger, bitterness, fear, guilt, or shame are all easier than forgiveness. Understand how to have compassion for yourself and others, how to have empathy with yourself and others and how to have forgiveness of yourself and others. The world is full of people who have been hurt in some way through being abandoned, abused, or accused. Find solid affirmations to change your story.

What questions will you ask yourself to determine your future relationships:

Conclusion

See your soul self and your ego self as two different beings. Live life in abundance through knowing that whatever you do you are helping others. Rise above your present thinking and the programming of your mind from outside influences, focus on your ultimate purpose and the pathway to reach it. Realize that when you have a spiritual awakening you are at one with everything. Remember, you cannot possess anything, you are merely a custodian of all things for the time you are alive, and the Earth needs you to connect with it. Align to have soul strength so you can eventually give yourself permission to die in good karma, knowing you have attempted to experience Heart Freedom and have no regrets, resentment or retribution from your life or relationships, and that you can die wholly in peace.

We run numerous relationship classes, events, one to one sessions, retreats, and workshops at event centers here in the UK and around the world. We also provide many retreat experiences at various venues around the world.

For further details please email: lionel@lionelpalatine.com

Reconnecting With Your True Self

We truly hope that you have enjoyed this journey and that our guides on how to achieve and experience a new relationship will help you achieve ecstatic joy and happiness.

To end this book, we have put together some resources to help you open your mind to new ways of thinking.

There are so many questions that need addressing before we can finally be free to live the lives we want to lead:

- When we want something in life, why do we so often do the opposite of what actually might let us attain it?
- Have you recognized a gaping hole in your life that needs to be filled by a caring, sharing partner?
- Do you assume you still haven't met the one? Or do you keep meeting the wrong sort of person to fulfil your desires?
- Have you ever considered that you might not have met the right person because you haven't been the right person?

No matter how many relationships we have, or may have had, the statistics for a happy congruent relationship don't bode well. In many ways, relationships seem harder than ever, even though we have more ways to communicate than ever before.

- Are we actually able and available to create a loving, committed and romantic union between two soul mates? Are we searching in the wrong places, asking the wrong questions, and just expecting a miraculous relationship to appear from thin air?
- Are you inwardly pining for something that seems outwardly unattainable? Do you complain - if only to yourself - about the lack of love in your life or even in

- your present relationship?
- Were you ever hurt or disappointed during childhood, in adolescence or as an adult and inwardly, perhaps not even consciously, are you still too scared to open your heart and be vulnerable and truly loved for fear of being hurt all over again?

There is a massive difference between wanting something and being ready to receive it into your life.

Are you committed to creating a truly romantic, loving, caring relationship even if it takes a lifetime of searching?

Allow us to help you set clear and attainable intentions of what you really want from your soul mate connection. Together let's create the space and the confidence in your ability to transform your life with the one and only relationship that will bring you truth, joy, and ultimate love.

The questions and the self-assessment to follow will challenge you to think deeply about yourself and your views on many different subjects.

Enjoy your inner exploration.

Dawn and Lionel xx

100 QUESTIONS

Before you complete your Lifestyle Self-Assessment Questionnaire on pages 281 to 301, we ask you to consider the following questions. They will allow you to open your mind and get to know yourself better. They will help you dream of the life you want to live. Take your time with them.

The key to living a truly ecstatic life full of joy, happiness and bliss is to really know who you are and to live authentically. You should live your truth and speak your truth.

1. What's the best compliment you've ever received?

2. What's one thing you're deeply proud of but would never put on your resumé?

3. What's the most out-of-character choice you've ever made?

4. If a mysterious benefactor wrote you a cheque for £5000 and said, "Help me solve a problem, any problem!" What would you do with him or her?

5. What's going to be carved on your (hypothetical) gravestone?

6. What are you freakishly good at?

7. What's one dream that you've tucked away? How come?

8. What are you starving for?

9. If you could have tea with one fictional character, who would it be?

10. Do you have a morning ritual? If so, what is it?

11. Do you believe in magic? When have you felt it?

12. Is there something that people consistently ask for your advice on? What is it?

13. Have you ever fantasized about changing your first name? To what?

14. When was the last time you astonished yourself?

15. What's your personal anthem or theme song?

16. Do you ever yearn for your life before Facebook?

17. What's your definition of an ideal houseguest?

18. If you had an extra £1000 to spend on yourself every week, what would you do?

19. If you could sit down with your 15-year old self, what would you tell him or her?

20. What are you bored of?

21. What's the best birthday cake you ever ate?

22. How do you engage with homeless people on the streets?

23. Do you think love is chemical, intellectual, spiritual, or completely undefinable?

24. Have you ever dreamed about starting a business? Or if you've already got one maybe a new business?

25. Are you afraid of flying in airplanes? How come?

26. What's your most urgent priority for the rest of the year?

27. If you could master any instrument on earth, what would it be?

28. Have you ever been genuinely afraid for your physical safety?

29. What are you an expert on? Is it because of training, lived experience, or both?

30. Has a teacher ever changed your life? How so?

31. Are there any household chores you secretly enjoy? Which ones and why?

32. How do you reign in self-critical voices?

33. If you could custom blend a perfume or cologne, what would it include?

34. What does fear feel like in your body?

35. Do you think you're currently operating at 100% capacity?

36. What do you value most: free time, recognition, or money?

37. If you could save one endangered species from extinction, which would you choose?

38. Are there any laws or social rules that completely baffle you?

39. Would you like to write a book? If so, about what?

40. If you could choose your own life obstacles, would you keep the ones you have?

41. Have you ever screamed at someone? What did they do?

42. Do you think there's going to be an anti-technology backlash in your lifetime?

43. Where and when do you get your best ideas?

44. Have you ever met one of your heroes?

45. What's in your fridge right this moment?

46. Can you tell when someone is lying?

47. Can you tell when someone is telling the truth?

48. Have you ever pushed your body further than you dreamed possible?

49. Are you living your life purpose or are you still searching?

50. Have you ever had to make a public apology? How come?

51. What's the worst piece of advice you've ever been given?

52. Do you think we're designed for monogamy? Why or why not?

53. How do you celebrate your victories?

54. Would you consider yourself an introvert, extrovert, or ambivert?

55. Do you ever hunt for answers or omens in dreams?

56. Do you think everyone has the capacity to be a leader?

57. Is war a necessary evil?

58. Are you a starter, a finisher, or an implementer?

59. Have you ever unplugged from the internet for more than a week?

60. Do you think we should live like we will die tomorrow?

61. Do you have any habits or quirks you wish you could erase?

62. What was the most agonizing hour of your life?

63. Have you ever dramatically changed a habit, or got yourself out of a rut? How did you do it?

64. Would you rather be a lonely genius, or a sociable idiot?

65. How would you fix the economy?

66. What was your very first job?

67. What brings you sheer delight?

68. Are you highly useful in a crisis?

69. Do you like to be saved or do you like to do the saving?

70. What's one mistake you keep repeating?

71. If you were heading out on a road trip right this minute, what would you pack?

72. Do you have any irrational fears?

73. When you see peers and competitors getting things you want; how do you react?

74. If you were to die three hours from now, what would you regret most?

75. What's something you've tried, that you'll never, ever try again?

76. If you could enroll in a PhD program, with your tuition paid in full by a mysterious benefactor, what would you study and why?

77. Have you ever had a complete and total nervous breakdown? How did you recuperate?

78. Have you ever set two friends up on a date? How did it go?

79. Have you ever questioned your faith — or lack thereof?

80. What's your recipe for recuperating from extreme heartbreak?

81. Have you ever had a psychic reading? Did you believe it? Was it accurate?

82. Have you ever kept a New Year's resolution?

83. Have you ever met someone who was genuinely evil?

84. Do you believe that everyone deserves redemption and forgiveness?

85. What was the best kiss of your entire life?

86. Do you prefer a printed book to an e-reader?

87. Do you have any physical features that you try to cloak or hide? How come?

88. What makes you so special anyway? No, really.

89. What's in your pocket (or purse, or man-bag) right now?

90. Do you ever fantasize about being in a rock band? What would your group be called?

91. What's your guiltiest of guilty pleasures?

92. Who's on your panel of imaginary mentors?

93. Have you ever stolen anything? Money, candy, hearts, time?

94. When was the last time you saw an animal in the wild?

95. What's the hardest thing you ever had to write and why?

96. Who's the last person that deeply disappointed you? What happened?

97. Have you ever won an award? What was it for?

98. How long can you (comfortably) go without checking your emails or texts? How do you feel about that?

99. What do you deserve and get to receive, no matter what?

100. What are you ready to set into motion, today?

Lifestyle Self-Assessment Questionnaire

The following exercise is designed to help you see a bigger picture of your present situation, your pathway to a more balanced lifestyle and the ultimate purpose of your life.

We regularly completed this exercise ourselves and use it in Life Wishes Workshops, to see how and where things are in or out of balance. Much as any of us may try to be in perfect harmony, life has its own agenda, and this simple exercise just makes us realize in which areas of our life we need to make alterations to become more rounded people.

Discipline yourself to regularly take half an hour out of your day to simply assess whether the things you are doing are adding to or taking away from your overall happiness. When you're in the right place to attract the things you want, the attraction won't be the hard thing at all.

Environmental Principles

1	Your Environment	To live, work and play in nurturing spaces.
2	Your Community	To serve and be part of your community.
3	Your Natural World	Do you respect the Earth our home?

Physical Health Principles

4	Your Diet	Nourishing your body with fresh, healthy food.
5	Your Daily Exercise	Having a fit and healthy body to live in.
6	Your Pure Physicality	Are you free of toxic chemicals?

Emotional Happiness Principles

7	Your Relationships with Family	Nourishing loving family relationships.
8	Your Intimate Relationship	Feelings of unconditional love and freedom.
9	Your Relationship with Yourself	Do you believe in yourself?

Spiritual Bliss Principles

10	Your Personality	Your authenticity - the real you.
11	Your Inner Nature	To have clear purpose and passion.
12	Your Beliefs	Are you living in harmony with your beliefs?

To assess your ability to attract anything into your life, simply answer the following questions with a YES or a NO answer. If you have any doubts, just answer what seems most true to you at this moment and to the best of your knowledge.

Lifestyle Self-Assessment Questionnaire

Be honest with yourself and think of all the things that you presently do in each area of your life and be guided by the questions asked.

Count the number of YES answers; your score for each section, then enter each section's score into the table towards the end of the assessment. Use the coloured wheel to mark a score for each section into a segment of the wheel to assess its roundness.

Then see how round is your wheel? The more round your wheel, the better it will roll, and the more fulfilled you will be in life. The bigger your wheel, the faster it will roll, and the sooner you will attract into your life the very things you desire most.

Let's begin. Your journey starts on the next page.

1. **Your Environment**

		YES	NO
1	Does your home and workspace inspire and support your wellbeing?		
2	Are your home and workspaces free from clutter?		
3	Are your home and work environments clean and fresh, do they smell good?		
4	Is your home and places of work in areas that uplift your spirit?		
5	Is your home and work environment free from invisible hazards such as EMF's, air pollution, noise disturbance etc.?		
6	Do you feel good in your home and workplaces, are they free from dominant, energy draining people?		
7	Do you have good natural light, fresh air and access to nature from within your home and workspaces?		
8	Do you have enough personal space within your home and work environments?		
9	Is your home and work environment a reflection of you and personalized?		
10	Is the Vibe (energetic flow) of your home and workspace right for you?		
	Total number of YES answers....		

Lifestyle Self-AssessmentQuestionnaire

2. Your Community

		YES	NO
1	Do you feel part of your community; do you feel a sense of belonging in the community in which you live?		
2	Do you feel like a valued member of the team where you work?		
3	Are you a member of another community or group that gives you a sense of belonging through your social life, spirituality, charity work, a society or class that you attend regularly?		
4	Do you feel cared for by your neighbours?		
5	Are you part of a network in your community that lets you know the welfare of others in your area (i.e. newsletter, parish news etc.)?		
6	Do you help look after the people in your community who are vulnerable or who have special needs?		
7	Do you take part in community action to resolve issues of your community?		
8	Do you help with community events?		
9	Do you share the values of your community and take responsibility for living / working in harmony with your neighbours?		
10	Do you feel able to contribute to your community in other meaningful ways?		
	Total number of YES answers….		

3. **Your Natural World**

		YES	NO
1	Do you recycle in your home?		
2	Do you avoid using toxic chemicals in your home, garden, and place of work?		
3	Do you avoid using a lot of electricity?		
4	Do you avoid using fuel for personal transport and use public transport whenever possible?		
5	Do you grow your own food or if not do you buy locally grown, in season, produce?		
6	Do you take an active part in the protection of wildlife and the environment either directly or through supporting organizations or charities that do?		
7	Do you get involved politically in lobbying for the protection of our environment?		
8	Do you conserve energy in any way that you can?		
9	Do you have a green policy at work or in your other projects regarding energy efficiency or recycling?		
10	Do you relate to the plants and animals around you consciously and compassionately, such as being a vegetarian/vegan etc?		
	Total number of YES answers		

Lifestyle Self-AssessmentQuestionnaire

4.   Your Diet

		YES	NO
1	Do you generally eat a healthy diet?		
2	Do you regularly eat your 5 fruit and vegetables per day?		
3	Do you eat plenty of fresh raw fruit and vegetables and natural fresh juices each day?		
4	Do you avoid adding salt to your food?		
5	Do you avoid stimulating drinks: tea, coffee, other caffeine drinks and alcohol?		
6	Do you avoid high calorie food such as sweets and crisps?		
7	Do you avoid sugar i.e. cakes, sweets and sweeteners in drinks?		
8	Do you avoid processed foods?		
9	Do you drink more than 2 litres of water a day?		
10	Do you avoid meat and dairy products?		
	Total number of YES answers		

5. Your Daily Exercise

		YES	NO
1	Are you free from aches and pains?		
2	Do you consider you have good posture?		
3	Do you flex your body daily?		
4	Do you get at least 30 minutes of fresh air and sunshine every day?		
5	Do you breathe deeply and evenly?		
6	Do you take regular physical exercise?		
7	Are you able to relax physically, letting go of stress easily?		
8	Do you get enough rest, and do you sleep well?		
9	Are you able to relax physically and let go of all tension before bed?		
10	Do you feel sexually fulfilled and satisfied?		
	Total number of YES answers		

Lifestyle Self-Assessment Questionnaire

6.   Your Pure Physicality

		YES	NO
1	Do you avoid non-prescription drugs?		
2	Do you limit your alcohol intake to less than the legal driving limit?		
3	Do you avoid smoking and being in the company of people that smoke?		
4	Are you at a healthy weight?		
5	Do you avoid exposing yourself to excessive sunlight?		
6	Do you avoid exposing yourself to sexually transmitted diseases?		
7	Do you avoid the use of drugs, preservatives and colours in foods and drinks?		
8	Do you avoid using toxic chemicals, being conscious of the chemicals in your shampoos, conditioners, soaps, household products etc.?		
9	Do you avoid being subject to excessive electromagnetic radiation such as microwave cooking, cordless phones etc. in your home?		
10	Are you happy with your lifestyle, do you consider it healthy?		
	Total number of YES answers		

7.   **Your Relationships with Family**

		YES	NO
1	Do you feel your childhood was loving and affectionate?		
2	Do you have loving supportive friends?		
3	Are your relationships free from abuse and neglect?		
4	Do you feel fulfilled in your closest relationship?		
5	Are you free of dominant people's needs past and present?		
6	Are you free from emotional neediness?		
7	Are you free from feelings of loneliness and isolation?		
8	Do you receive enough cuddles and affection?		
9	Are you able to express your love freely?		
10	Do you receive unconditional love and attention?		
	Total number of YES answers		

Lifestyle Self-Assessment Questionnaire

8.   Your Intimate Relationship

		YES	NO
1	Are you content with your present relationship?		
2	Does your relationship satisfy you and is it in harmony with your values?		
3	Do you balance your relationship with work and play?		
4	Do you dedicate time, energy, and money to your relationship?		
5	Is your relationship satisfactory or are you striving for perfection?		
6	Are you free from anxiety in your relationship?		
7	Do you feel able to cope with your relationship without other needs like drink or drugs?		
8	Do your primary relationships free you from fear and insecurity?		
9	Do your relationships keep you free from stress?		
10	Does your sex life satisfy you emotionally and physically?		
	Total number of YES answers		

9. Your Relationship with Yourself

		YES	NO
1	Are you free from physical illness and symptoms of emotional baggage?		
2	Can you think clearly and work effectively?		
3	Do you avoid indulging in excessive food, alcohol or drugs?		
4	Can you avoid becoming demeaning or aggressive towards yourself?		
5	Are you able to communicate your feelings effectively?		
6	Are you free from past feelings of lost trust, great disappointment, shame, guilt or fear?		
7	Are you able to tell the person you are in an intimate relationship with how you are feeling?		
8	Are you able to be angry with people?		
9	Are you able to cry in the presence of others?		
10	Do you express your emotions freely?		
	Total number of YES answers		

Lifestyle Self-AssessmentQuestionnaire

10. Your Personality

		YES	NO
1	Does your work and home uplift your energy?		
2	Do you avoid stress and anxiety to keep your energy up?		
3	Do you feel you have plenty of energy?		
4	Do you replenish your energy with a balanced lifestyle (rest, exercise, and proper nutrition)?		
5	Do you avoid taking on too much and share the workload with others?		
6	Do you avoid losing energy through excesses of food, drink, and drugs?		
7	Do you lift your energy with lots of creativity and intimacy?		
8	Do you avoid energy zappers (emotionally draining people)?		
9	Do you avoid giving too much emotionally in relationships past and present?		
10	Do you ask for help when tired or in difficult situations?		
	Total number of YES answers		

11. Your Inner Nature

		YES	NO
1	Do you live your life based on your own values and needs?		
2	Does your life and work excite you?		
3	Are you true to yourself?		
4	Do you project a genuine image of yourself?		
5	Are you able to fully express yourself creatively?		
6	Are you committed to finding a better path in life?		
7	Are you currently reaching your full potential for happiness?		
8	Does your life have meaning for you?		
9	Are you on the right path to fulfil your purpose?		
10	Do you love yourself and the life you have created?		
	Total number of YES answers		

Lifestyle Self-AssessmentQuestionnaire

12.   Your Beliefs

		YES	NO
1	Do you express free spirit and joyfulness in your life?		
2	Can you find and maintain inner peace?		
3	Do you ask for help through prayer, spiritual guidance or your god?		
4	Are you spiritually aware enough to face your own death or loss of a loved one?		
5	Are you able to tune into any source of communication or meditation?		
6	Are you able to use your visualization and affirmations to be creative?		
7	Are you able to assess your own spiritual values and true beliefs?		
8	Is your inner spiritual strength strong enough to protect you from negativity?		
9	Do you have good sources of spiritual alignment you can tap into?		
10	Do you take time out each day for regular spiritual practice?		
	Total number of YES answers		

Your Scores

Environmental Principles

	Subject	Description	Score
1	My Environment	I live, work and play in nurturing spaces.	
2	My Community	I serve and be part of your community.	
3	Your Natural World	I respect the Earth our home.	

Physical Health Principles

	Subject	Description	Score
4	My Diet	I nourish my body with fresh healthy food.	
5	My Daily Exercise	I have a fit and healthy body to live in.	
6	Your Pure Physicality	I am free of toxic chemicals?	

Emotional Happiness Principles

	Subject	Description	Score
7	My Relationships with Family	Nourishing loving family relationships.	
8	My Intimate Relationship	I feel unconditionally loved and free.	
9	My Relationship with Yourself	I believe in myself	

Spiritual Bliss Principles

	Subject	Description	Score
10	My Personality	My authenticity - the real me.	
11	My Inner Nature	I have clear purpose and passion.	
12	My Beliefs	Are you living in harmony with your beliefs?	

Lifestyle Self-Assessment Questionnaire

Lifestyle Wheel

Now to visualize your Lifestyle Self-Assessment exercise. Enter each of your scores into the individual segments of the wheel (representing the 12 principles), counting outwards from the centre (the centre being zero and the outer circle being 10) by putting a dark line indicating your score on the relevant line of the segment. This will represent the number you have scored on that principle.

To feel completely fulfilled, your wheel will be scoring 10 on each segment. Please review your circle and assess the segments with the lowest scores i.e. the marks closest to the centre of the circle.

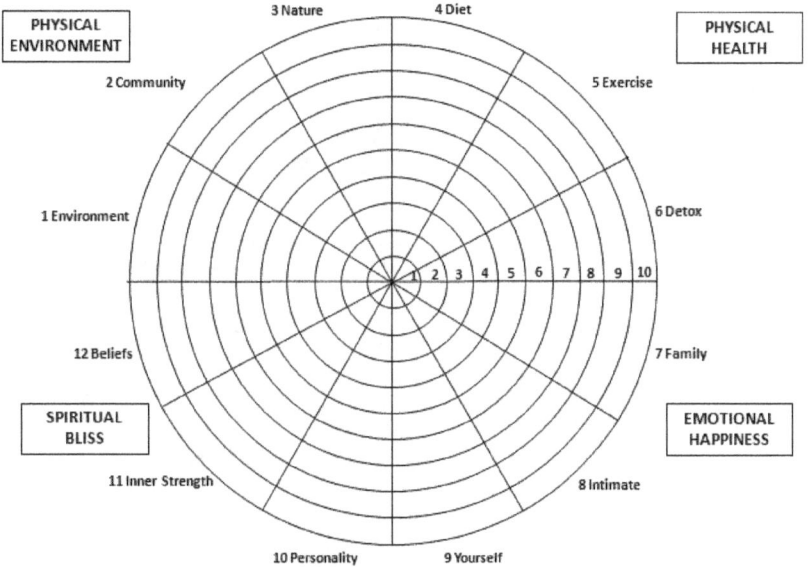

BELIEVE IN LOVE

Now it is time to work on your low sectors, so you can enrich your life with happiness, and make any necessary changes to attract unconditional love, joy, and ecstatic happiness into your life.

Let's look at making an action plan to bring about the changes that will make a real difference in your life, and the lives of people around you. Using the three lowest scoring principles fill out the following pages and take action to bring about your personal joy.

Lifestyle Self-AssessmentQuestionnaire

My Action Plan – My Personal Priorities

Priority One

Address the Lowest Scoring Segment: -

What is my first objective?

What help do I need to achieve my objective?

What information do I need to find out to fulfil my objective?

What actions do I need to take and by when?

Who will my actions affect?

What do I need to communicate and to whom?

How will I do it?

What help will I need to do it?

Lifestyle Self-Assessment Questionnaire

Priority Two

Address the Second Lowest Scoring Segment: -

What is my first objective?

What help do I need to achieve my objective?

What information do I need to find out to fulfil my objective?

What actions do I need to take and by when?

Who will my actions affect?

What do I need to communicate and to whom?

How will I do it?

What help will I need to do it?

Lifestyle Self-Assessment Questionnaire

Priority Three

Address the Third Lowest Scoring Segment: -

What is my first objective?

What help do I need to achieve my objective?

What information do I need to find out to fulfil my objective?

What actions do I need to take and by when? Who will my actions affect?

What do I need to communicate and to whom?

How will I do it?

What help will I need to do it?

Congratulations!

Congratulations on completing your Lifestyle Self-Assessment and creating your personal priority plan to bring health, harmony, and happiness into your life. This is such an inspirational way to bring balance and harmony into your life and to enrich your mind, body, and soul.

Now it is time to commit to accomplishing your goals with a friend who can support you and who you can support in return.

My Supporter is:

I commit to:

Signed Date

Lifestyle Self-AssessmentQuestionnaire

We sincerely thank you for reading this book, for delving into our inner world and joining us on our journey to health, wealth, and happiness. This is such a special journey for all, we hope your lives and the lives you touch benefit from it.

The End
(Or is it the beginning?)

With love, respect, appreciation and gratitude from Dawn and Lionel xx

BELIEVE IN LOVE

Glossary of Terms

Aura	The distinctive individual atmosphere or quality that is generated by a person.
Auric	Pertaining to the Aura.
Auric Field	The size or reach of the Aura.
Bliss	Perfect happiness; great joy. "She gave a sigh of bliss" *Synonyms:* joy, pleasure, delight, happiness, gladness, ecstasy, elation, rapture, euphoria, heaven, paradise, seventh heaven, cloud nine, utopia, Eden, Arcadia; halcyon days. *Informal:* the top of the world - "it was sheer bliss to be there"
Blissland	Heaven on Earth. A place where we all want to live, a better world. The name of Lionel and Dawn's sacred events centre in Cheshire, England that harvested happiness.
Feng Shui	Feng Shui also known as Chinese geomancy, is pseudoscience originating from ancient China, which claims to use energy forces to harmonize individuals with their surrounding environment.[1] The term *Feng Shui* literally translates as "wind-water" in English

Five Elements	Feng Shui practice holds that all things consist of varying degrees of the <u>five elements</u>: wood, fire, earth, metal, and water. Each is represented by certain colours that can help you bring harmony to a particular space. The five elements can interact in any number of ways, some constructive and some destructive. In the constructive cycle, for example, water provides moisture for trees (wood) to grow; wood then becomes a fuel for fire; the residue of fire is ash or soil; the ash/soil is the essence of earth minerals that form metals; and as metal cool, they allow water to condense, completing the cycle. In a destructive cycle, on the other hand, metal can cut wood; and wood can grow over and consume soil, water can extinguish fire, earth can absorb water.
Sex	(Chiefly with reference to people) sexual activity, including specifically sexual intercourse. "They enjoyed talking about sex" *Synonym:* sexual intercourse, intercourse, lovemaking, making love, sex act, sexual relations, sexual/vaginal/anal penetration; mating; rumpy pumpy, coitus, coition, copulation. "a group of teenage boys sat around the table talking about sex" the facts of life, sexual reproduction, reproduction, the birds, and the bees have sexual intercourse (with), make love (to), sleep with/together, go to bed with/together, mate (with); seduce, ravish; get one's oats, be intimate (with)

Glossary of Terms

Spirit	The non-physical part of a person which is the seat of emotions and character, the soul. "We seek a harmony between body and spirit" *Synonyms:* soul, psyche, inner self, inner being, essential being pneuma, anima, ego, id, ka, atman The prevailing or typical quality, mood, or attitude of a person, group, or period of time. "I hope the team will build on this **spirit of confidence**" *Synonyms* ethos, prevailing tendency, motivating force, animating principle, dominating characteristic, essence, quintessence. atmosphere, mood, feeling, temper, tenor, climate. attitudes, beliefs, principles, standards, ethics "The spirit of the nineteenth century"
Tribe	A social division in a traditional society consisting of families or communities linked by social, economic, religious, or blood ties, with a common culture and dialect, for example, indigenous Indian tribes/the nomadic tribes of the Sahara. *Synonyms:* ethnic group, people, race, nation, family, dynasty; house, clan
Vibe	A person's emotional state or the atmosphere of a place as communicated to and felt by others. "we've been picking up some **good vibes** on that guy".
Vibrat-ions	A person's emotional state, the atmosphere of a place, or the associations of an object, as communicated to and felt by others.
Yin & Yang	The core theory of yin and yang is the belief that a balance of the feminine (yin) and the masculine

(yang) is necessary to maintain a good flow of energy to create a healthy happy, fulfilling, successful life.

In Taoist and Feng Shui theory, yin and yang are opposites that are dependent upon one another, and which must always be in balance. The principle of duality—the idea that all things are balanced blends of two things—is at the root of yin/yang theory. While most other spiritual philosophies believe in opposing dualities, such as good vs. evil, the Chinese Taoist system believes that balance and equilibrium between opposites is the desirable state. Discord occurs when one principle outweighs the other.

Glossary of Terms

References within the book:

Self-Discovery Personality Profiling Tool
lionel@lionelpalatine.com

The Seven Spiritual Laws of Success by Deepak Chopra
www.chopra.com

Expert Space Clearer by Beverley Wood
www.thehealthyhousearchitect.com

Five Languages of Love by Gary Chapman
www.5lovelanguages.com

Spiritual University Centres - Brahma Kumaris
www.brahmakumaris.org

Fivelements Resort
www.fivelements.org

Kamalaya - Koh Samui's Emotional Detox Programme
www.kamalaya.com

Meditation Techniques
www.thebrightpath.com

Coby Zvikler - Empower Disc
www.empowerdisc.co.uk

Giselle Rufer
www.delance.com

Creating Sacred Space by Karen Kingston
www.spaceclearing.com

Clear Your Clutter with Feng Shui by Karen Kingston
www.spaceclearing.com

Unleash the Power Within by Anthony Robbins
www.tonyrobbins.com

Feng Shui Society of Great Britain
www.fengshuisociety.org.uk

Feng Shui - Simon Brown
www.chienergy.co.uk

Harmonious Solutions - Elizabeth Well
www.harmonious-solutions.co.uk

Feng Shui - Richard Ashworth
www.imperialfengshui.info

Spiritual Healing - Alison Levesley
www.alisonlevesley.com

Ubud Village Hotel, Bali
www.theubudvillage.com

The Yoga Barn, Ubud, Bali
www.theyogabarn.com

British Society of Dowsers
www.britishdowsers.org

Ayduvedic Retreat, Ubud, Bali
www.amrtasiddhi.com

T. Harv Eker
www.harveker.com

Divining Cards by Dr Steven Farmer
www.drstevenfarmer.com

Divining Cards by Alana Fairchild
www.alanafairchild.com

Divining Cards by Lionel Palatine
lionel@lionelpalatine.com

The Golden Circle by Simon Sinek
www.simonsinek.com

Glossary of Terms

Seven Questions to Find Your Life's Passion

Answer the following questions to uncover your life's passion and your purpose should flow from the answers.

These questions are the same as the Seven Steps to Success seen earlier in this book. Dawn and Lionel share their own answers over the following pages.

1. What have been the greatest moments of joy and fulfilment in your life?

2. What are the greatest sources of joy in your career?

3. What activities do you absolutely love in your personal life?

4. What are your greatest talents and natural abilities?

5. What is the single most important thing you would like to accomplish in your career?

6. What is the one most important thing you would like to achieve in your life?

7. What is the relationship between all the answers to those questions?

Glossary of Terms

Lionel Palatine

Lionel David Palatine is a keen writer, business owner, investor, consultant, and relationship guide.

Born: 29th July 1959, Manchester
Late spouse: Dr. Dawn De Vivre MBE.

As someone who found financial freedom early in life, I am now able to spend my time helping others find fulfilment in their own lives. My mission is to help people create a healthier happier world for themselves.

BELIEVE IN LOVE

Far from teaching the methodologies I adopted for acquiring wealth, I have moved into consulting, guiding, and helping both individuals and couples with their relationships. I find this work far more rewarding than anything I ever achieved through any business.

When your relationships are right you can achieve anything you want. When you are happy, everything just falls into place naturally. I do this work because it fulfils my sense of purpose and I like to see happy people and live in a positive and abundant world full of love.

I use three reflective programs to help people become more of the person they want to be. I help individuals to find their emotional freedom, I guide couples to find or reignite their relationship passions, and I teach groups to find happiness through their spiritual connection. You can find out more about these programs on lionel@lionelpalatine.com

I also have a devotion to build a healthier happier environment through using less, recycling and reusing the resources we already have. I still run two property businesses so I can also help with wealth creation for those in need of support.

Lionel is father of one daughter and one son, and presently grandfather to one beautiful little girl.

Contact Lionel on lionel@lionelpalatine.com

Glossary of Terms

Lionel reveals his answers to the seven questions:

1. **What have been the greatest moments of joy and fulfilment in your life?**

The births and parenting of my two children.
Connecting with love and finding fulfilling relationships. Appreciating all I have, especially my first grandchild. The freedom of running my own businesses for over 40 years. Meditation, connection and being inspired to run workshops.

2. **What are the greatest sources of joy in your career?**

Having the freedom to choose what I do, when and why. Guiding couples to reunite and reignite the flame of love. Advising people how to succeed in their own wealth creation. Training people to find their own freedom, value, and to understand themselves.
Helping people to find their own opportunities and help themselves create a better future.

3. **What activities do you absolutely love in your personal life?**

Being in nature when its warm and dry.
Having an energetic connection with people in love. Connecting with what I know as sacred energy. Competitive social evenings like bridge or quiz nights. Fixing and repairing things, upcycling, building, mechanics.

4.   What are your greatest talents and natural abilities?

The determination and willingness to complete tasks.
I'm a practical thinker, systemized and organized.
The practical ability to work with my hands.
Connecting with the energy of nature. Self-expression through writing.

5.   What is the single most important thing you would like to accomplish in your career?

Help more people to help themselves find harmony and balance in their life.

6.   What is the one most important thing you would like to achieve in your life?

Just to be happy and fulfilled from my actions.

7.   What is the relationship between all the answers to those questions?

My daily practice for emotional freedom, physical health, and spiritual joy.

Glossary of Terms

Dr. Dawn De Vivre MBE

Dr. Dawn De Vivre MBE was an author, teacher, speaker, and gifted storyteller

Born 5th June 1958, Macclesfield, Cheshire
Husband: Lionel David Palatine.

Dr Dawn De Vivre MBE was once voted more influential than Sir Richard Branson and James Dyson, as well as Veuve Clicquot 'Business Woman of the Year'. She founded, built, and sold her global manufacturing company for millions and has appeared on the Channel 4 programme *The Secret Millionaire twice*.

Dawn was a woman who dares to be different, she used Feng

Shui to transform herself and her global manufacturing business from a half million-pound loss to a five-million- pound profit in 3 years, increasing team happiness from 60% to 90% at the same time.

Universities across the UK awarded Dawn Doctorates for her tireless passion to empower people, make a difference and create a better world.

Dawn was a vibrant public speaker inspiring global audiences with her colourful, creative, courageous style.

Dawn was mother of two daughters, grandmother of four, she lived in Cheshire with her soul mate Lionel Palatine.

Dawn reveals her answers to the seven questions: -

1. **What have been the greatest moments of joy and fulfilment in your life?**

The birth and love for two daughters and seeing them following their truth.
Becoming a Grandma to one granddaughter and three grandsons.
The pure joy experienced at 12.12pm on 12.12.12 at Matamanoa, Fiji where Lionel, my soul mate, asked me to spend the rest of my life with him.

2. **What are the greatest sources of joy in your career?**

Creating a company with my dad and knowing he died happy as we were on our way to sensational success.
Being awarded MBE and Pioneer of the Life of our Nation by HRH the Queen.
Being awarded Honorary Doctorates from Manchester, Staffordshire and Chester Universities.
Creating a global brand for Flowcrete with Feng Shui and

Glossary of Terms

teamwork (500 staff).
Transforming Flowcrete from £500,000 loss to £5m profit with Feng Shui, 5S and teamwork.
Being able to say 'yes' to a little child and create a trail of giant bears (Bearmania) in Congleton – going global in the Financial Times (my dad would have been proud).
The Spirit of Margaret Williamson coming through to me at Congleton Spiritualist Church and telling me my role here on the planet is to 'Teach the children what they don't teach in schools.'

3. **What activities do you absolutely love in your personal life?**

Sensual tantric connection with my soul mate Lionel, every minute connected to Lionel.
Playing with my grandchildren - being a magical child with them.
Walking in nature with Lionel, my children, and their children.
Attending my daughter's yoga classes - just feeling the pure joy of her joy.

Family Holidays laughing and having big fun together.
Ritual, Ceremony, Atmospheric Cleansing, Home Blessings.
Sharing Lionel's and my story with strangers.
Running in nature, connecting with the buzzards.
My morning spiritual gratitude, ritual, and chanting mantras.

4. **What are your greatest talents and natural abilities?**

I am a Visionary, Enthusiastic Champion of Change.
Motivational Speaker and Storyteller.
My creativity – idea generation.
I am an Artist
Purpose Passion and Power Personality Profiling.
Connecting likeminded souls to make a difference. Teamwork and hosting gatherings.

Divining with crystals, rods, cards, and my body. Dowsing for geopathic stress and ley lines.
Healthy Happy Home and business surveys.
Atmospheric Cleansing and Blessing.
Hosting, guiding, entertaining and teaching.

5.   What is the single most important thing you would like to accomplish in your career?

Create 'joie de vivre pour tout le monde' - joy of living for all the world.
Bring balance and inner happiness to billions by mass awareness of our personality profiling tool.
I'd like to teach the world to live in perfect harmony.

6.   What is the one most important thing you would like to achieve in your life?

In 2050, knowing 50% of humanity is vibrating at over 500 on the David Hawkin's Consciousness Scale due to a contribution from Lionel, myself, my children, my children's children and all the likeminded souls we have worked with to raise the vibration of humanity to the vibration of love.

To die happy, pass over to heaven in complete tantric peaceful bliss in the arms of my soul mate Lionel when I'm 94 and he is 93 at 12.12pm on the 12$^{th\ of}$ December 2052.

7.   What is the relationship between all the answers to those questions?

The key to happiness is to find your inner nature, connect with nature, live naturally and to be your natural self & you will BELIVE IN LOVE & experience unconditional pure love.

Offerings

Dawn passed away on 11th February 2022 after an eight-month battle with cancer. She died peacefully in Lionel's arms as she had hoped to. Through the Last Wishes program (www.lastwishes.world) they had planned the details of her natural burial and the hopes and intentions of Dawn's vision of the legacy she would leave to her family, her friends, and the community she loved so much.

Even though her life was taken at an age that many would perceive as too young, she was able to pass forward the love she felt for Lionel so that he would appreciate so much of what they had learned together. Life is but a fleeting moment in cosmic time, we must praise, respect and give gratitude for everything as well as understand the compassion, the empathy, and the value of the forgiveness that is true love.

BELIEVE IN LOVE

www.ingramcontent.com/pod-product-compliance
Lightning Source LLC
Chambersburg PA
CBHW071957220426
43662CB00009B/1162